"Sandy is pioneering mind–body detox."

THE TIMES

Other Books By Sandy C. Newbigging

Thunk!
How to Think Less for Serenity and Success

Life Detox
Clear Physical and Emotional Toxins
from Your Body and Your Life

Life-Changing Weight Loss
3 Steps to Get the Body and Life You Want

New Beginnings
10 Teachings to Make the Rest
of Your Life the Best of Your Life

STOP TREATING SYMPTOMS & INSTEAD...

HEAL
THE HIDDEN
CAUSE

USING THE 5-STEP MIND DETOX METHOD

SANDY C. NEWBIGGING

FINDHORN PRESS

4/13 16⁹⁵ + 1⁸⁵ pbk cv. B+T

DISCLAIMER

The medical information and all procedures mentioned and contained in this book are not intended to be used or construed as a substitute for professional medical care and advice provided by a physician. People who read this book and make decisions regarding their health or medical care, which they believe are based on ideas contained in this book, do so at their own risk. The author or publishers are making no medical claims. The author and publishers are not responsible for any adverse effects or consequences resulting from the use of any of the suggestions or information contained in this book, but offer this material as information, which the public has a right to hear and utilize at its own discretion. The author or publishers are making no medical claims. The author and publishers are not responsible for any adverse effects or consequences resulting from the use of any of the suggestions or information contained in this book, but offer this material as information which the public has a right to hear and utilize at its own discretion.

PRIVACY PROTECTION

Case study "success stories" have been gathered from the author's consultation notes between 2005 and 2012 and from the case notes of independent Mind Detox Method (MDM) practitioners. Client names have been changed to respect privacy. All case studies from independent MDM practitioners have been used with gratitude and on faith that they accurately reported the outcomes. Wordings of comments have been edited slightly for readability purposes only.

This book is dedicated to the growing team of Mind Detox Practitioners from around the world. You inspire me.

PROPERTY OF
LIBRARY OF THE CHATHAMS
CHATHAM NJ

© Sandy C. Newbigging, 2013

The right of Sandy C. Newbigging to be identified as the
author of this work has been asserted by him in accordance
with the Copyright, Designs and Patents Act 1998.

Published in 2013 by Findhorn Press, Scotland

ISBN 978-1-84409-614-5

All rights reserved.

The contents of this book may not be reproduced in any form,
except for short extracts for quotation or review,
without the written permission of the publisher.

A CIP record for this title is available from the British Library.

Edited by Jacqui Lewis
Cover design by Sandy Newbigging and Richard Crookes
Interior design by Damian Keenan
Printed and bound in the EU

Published by
Findhorn Press
117-121 High Street,
Forres IV36 1AB,
Scotland, UK

t +44 (0)1309 690582
f +44 (0)131 777 2711
e info@findhornpress.com
www.findhornpress.com

Contents

Miracle or Method?

· · · ·

DISCOVERING THE POWER OF
MAKING PEACE WITH THE PAST

A FEW YEARS AGO I WAS INVITED TO WORK AS A THERAPIST ON A DETOX HEALTH RETREAT IN SOUTHERN SPAIN. With no idea of what to expect (at that time I thought detox was only for drug addicts!), I packed my bag and headed off for a week in the sun. It rained heavily the entire time! I'm not sure if it was the lack of sun that week or what, but my therapy schedule quickly became fully booked.

In more ways than just the location, I found myself in unfamiliar territory. Many of the detoxers were investing in their health because they were suffering from physical problems. That week I was to meet people suffering with migraines, irritable bowel syndrome (IBS), infertility, bulimia, obesity and psoriasis. This meant that not only was I suddenly working in the field of 'health', but also, due to my schedule, that I only had a couple of hours with each of them.

A Fortunate Coincidence

Two weeks prior to going to Spain I had been invited to a talk by a specialist in the mind–body connection called Dr David Hamilton. During that inspiring talk (come to think of it, on another very wet day, this time just outside Glasgow), he shared many scientific studies that have investigated the power of the mind, including the mind's ability to heal the body.

With his message springing to the forefront of my own mind that day in Spain, I knew I had to update my therapeutic approach, fast. I suggested to my first client that we explore whether there might be any mental or emotional issues from their past that could be causing their physical problems today. With their agreement we proceeded.

Hmmm, To My Next Question...

I had no idea what to ask! I remember looking down at my blank notebook and then up again to meet the expectant eyes of my client. I decided to keep it simple by asking if there was an event in her life that might be causing her health condition, such that if we were to resolve it, the body would heal.

To both of our amazements, she immediately had an answer; a specific event had just "popped into her mind". With only a few more questions, we could see a possible link between the past emotional event and the current physical condition. Once we had established the possible cause, we worked on releasing any negative emotions associated with it and the session was done.

The Healing Power Of Peace

Time after time, in session after session, this happened with great success. Over the coming months I regularly witnessed instantaneous remissions from health conditions; I saw skin conditions clear up, chronic pain vanish, and digestion problems disappear, to name but a few. Along with this, I also witnessed the healing of many other emotional issues and life problems – all from helping people to make peace with their past.

Lucky Break

News about my method, which by this point was becoming known as "Mind Detox", then spread internationally when I was shown on three separate television series documenting people going through a mind–body detox retreat. The TV exposure and subsequent book deals led to the opportunity of working with hundreds of people at my clinics, workshops and retreats around the world.

It's a Miracle! (Or Is It?)

Over time I became curious. Was I bearing witness to miracles? Was I some kind of gifted healer? Or had I simply stumbled across a method of healing that could be transferable and used by others?

For the next year I started using the same therapeutic questions when working with clients at my clinics and retreats. Very quickly it became clear that the power of the method was the method itself, and the possibility of training others was real. Soon after I had realized this, I ran my first Mind Detox Masterclass and Practitioner Certification Course and started training people from around the world via my academy.

Using the Mind Detox Method to Heal

The Mind Detox Method is a very effective way to discover and heal the hidden causes of physical, emotional and life problems. Quite simply, if something negative is happening in your body or your life and you don't know why, then this method can help. By making peace with your past, chronic stress is reduced, allowing the body to heal, and by clearing your self-limiting beliefs, you can use your mind as the incredible tool that it is to create the life you want. It's a genuine win-win. So be courageous and go for it. The possibilities are truly infinite!

Sandy C. Newbigging
January 2013

Curing the Incurable

• • • •

BY SASHA ALLENBY, BEST-SELLING
AUTHOR OF *MATRIX REIMPRINTING USING EFT*

When I started out on my own journey of transforming two incurable long-term health conditions, I had no concept of the role that healing my underlying emotional issues would play in my return to health. Despite an open mind and an interest in holistic therapies, at the time of my sickness, I was still locked in the current popular western medical paradigm that something had gone 'wrong' with my body, that it had 'failed' me in some way, and that I needed some kind of outside intervention to 'fix' it. I didn't make even a tenuous link between the myriad life stresses, left unresolved and pushed down while I wore a mask of happiness on the surface, and the breakdown in my physiology. Despite trying a whole host of physical interventions spanning several years, it wasn't until I addressed the underlying emotional causative factors of my disease that my body healed, and when it did, the change was dramatic.

From Bed-Bound to Brilliant Health

The fact that I went from complete bed-bound disability to total health in a relatively short space of time may seem miraculous, but what I have witnessed and supported in others since actually makes it seem quite commonplace to me now. Inspired by my own transformation, and passionately wanting to share what I had learned, I went on to build an international client base, supporting thousands worldwide through my own practice and training courses. I also co-authored a book with the creator of a technique built on the very foundations that *Heal the Hidden Cause* rests upon: resolve the underlying emotional factors to a physical condition, and the body heals accordingly.

Time and again I saw people from all walks of life turn around a whole host of physiological and psychological conditions, or at least gain a vast improvement in their symptoms, when they addressed the specific underlying emotional factors to physical diseases, alongside the accompanying beliefs that were holding their body in a diseased state. I saw people transform everything from cancer to diabetes, bipolar affective disorder to chronic fatigue syndrome, rheumatoid arthritis, to post-traumatic stress disorder, eczema to phobias, to name but a few, until eventually the miraculous became normalized.

Simple Solution for Remarkable Results

Throughout this journey I have always been interested in creating, developing and researching tools and techniques that enable quick and lasting shifts in the emotional climate, and which enable the body and mind to return to a healthful state. So it was with great interest that I was introduced to Sandy C. Newbigging's Mind Detox Method. For me, one of the key factors underlying the success of this method is its simplicity. This makes it highly accessible to both practitioners who want to help their clients quickly uncover the root cause of a condition and to lay people who want to get to the heart of their own challenges. But don't be fooled by the simplicity of this method. The results of this technique are remarkable, and can be seen time and again in Sandy's thousands of clinical hours with clients.

Mind Detox Method is more than just another technique to transform the emotions; Sandy has built a whole system based on working with real people and the challenges that they face. So *Heal the Hidden Cause* does far more than deliver a technique for transformation and self-help. What I have experienced in my own practice and with the countless practitioners I have trained is that it is one thing to present a technique, but another thing altogether to address the deep underlying blocks that people face when they are using this technique to create changes for themselves. *Heal the Hidden Cause* does just that, not only presenting an accessible system that can be used by all but also highlighting a whole host of solutions to the blocks that people encounter when they are making personal changes.

There are some real gems in this book, from the in-depth exploration of how to identify and resolve the underlying core beliefs that are contributing to sickness and disease, to the blind-spot-busting, which highlights common blocking beliefs to creating transformation and how to move through them.

A Genuinely Helpful Self-Help Book

Heal the Hidden Cause is a book that is beneficial to all. It is for practitioners who want to support a deeper healing journey with their clients. Its accessibility also makes it the book that practitioners can give to their clients so they can better understand their own healing journey. It can also be given to a friend or a relative to demonstrate how they can impact their own healing. Perhaps most importantly, it is the book that you can use on yourself time and time again, as you deepen your understanding of how your mind and body are linked and put the tools in this book into practice on yourself. If you not only read this book but also consistently apply the Mind Detox Method to yourself, it can enable you to join the many ranks of people who have experienced the miraculous in their healing journey by addressing their unresolved emotional challenges. I wish you peace as your journey with Mind Detox Method unfolds.

Sasha Allenby
October 2012

*"Healing is a matter of time,
but it is also a matter of opportunity."*

HIPPOCRATES

Stop Treating Symptoms

• • • •

THE BODY DOESN'T BREAK
AND LIFE ISN'T AGAINST YOU

ENHANCED HEALTH, WEALTH AND HAPPINESS IS NOT SOME FAR-OFF FANTASY. Instead, it is your birthright as a human being. It is your most natural state of being because it takes effort, stress and being out of balance to live in any other way.

> *It is the natural tendency of the body to heal itself, and it will do so when given the chance.*

Using the methods outlined in this book I regularly witness physical healings occurring, along with dramatic improvements in how people feel and the life results they enjoy — all by doing one thing: helping people to heal their unhealthy beliefs by making peace with their past.

A Proven Method that Works Fast

Through my work as a therapist at clinics, workshops and residential retreats around the world, I have developed a method that enables people to discover and resolve the often hidden mental and emotional causes of physical conditions, emotional issues and life problems.

My method finds what I refer to as the Root-Cause Reason (RCR), which, as you will learn, is justifying the existence of one or more unhealthy beliefs. It then helps you to heal these unhealthy beliefs by coming to some healthier conclusions that, due to the interconnection between your mind, your body and your world, can cause healing to occur naturally in your body and your life.

Having tracked the main beliefs causing imbalances in hundreds of clients, I have discovered and worked with the most common unhealthy beliefs. In this book, I will share what these beliefs are so that you can make sure you don't have any of them – or if you do, so that you can heal them for improved health, wealth and happiness.

Move Beyond Treating Symptoms

Conventional approaches to healing physical conditions can fail to deliver long-term benefits because they often only treat the surface-level physical symptoms rather than healing the deeper underlying mental and emotional causes.

Ignoring the underlying causes is a bit like attempting to flatten a turbulent river without first removing the jagged rocks sitting below the surface; you can try all you like, but without removing the rocks it's going to make very little difference!

The mind and body are very much one. As a result, physical problems don't necessarily have purely physical causes. Due to the scientifically proven mind–body connection, mental beliefs and emotional unease can show up as physical problems too.

When you change your mind, your body responds accordingly, because the mind and body are in constant communication.

Millions of people unintentionally block their health, wealth and happiness with hidden unhealthy beliefs that are harmful to their bodies and lives. These beliefs put their bodies under unnecessary stress, which makes them more prone to experiencing physical "dis-ease". Incredibly, these beliefs also communicate with the individual cells of the body, which, as you will learn, can respond by creating physical conditions that mirror the consistent messages sent to them by the mind. Furthermore, beliefs influence how you interpret life events, thus also determining whether you experience a problematic or a peacefully productive life.

The body doesn't just break, and life isn't against you.

Your body is programmed for survival and will do everything it can to stay alive. In fact, I'd suggest it already is doing so! What you may consider to be a physical problem is in fact your body's best attempt at adapting in order to survive the mental and emotional conditions that it is subjected to in daily life.

If you have a problematic health condition then there is a reason why. Your body will simply keep creating the same problem until the reason for the condition is resolved. By resolving the underlying reasons why your problem has existed up until now, your problem simply has no alternative but to disappear for good. It just makes sense.

In my experience, the cause of many physical, emotional and life problems exist within the more subtle (unconscious) realms of the mind. They are usually hidden unhealthy beliefs that you are unaware even exist. This can make them very difficult to find and fix – unless you know how. With this book I share a proven method for doing exactly this, so that you can be free from your unhealthy beliefs for good.

ABOUT THIS BOOK

HEAL THE HIDDEN CAUSE is divided into three parts:

PART ONE: **The Healing Mindset**
PART TWO: **Discover the Hidden Cause**
PART THREE: **Heal the Hidden Cause**

IN PART ONE, I will introduce the idea of why enjoying better health, peace of mind and happiness is your birthright, share some inspiring real-life success stories and reveal my seven self-healing secrets. Knowing these secrets can help you to harness your own self-healing capabilities and cultivate the right mindset for healing your body, emotions and life.

IN PART TWO, I then help you to discover any unhealthy beliefs that might be secretly making you sick, making you feel bad or creating negative life situations. To make things easy for you, I share the most common unhealthy beliefs that I've come across, along with a simple yet powerful process for becoming aware of your own unconscious beliefs.

IN PART THREE, we turn our attention to resolution. Once you find your unhealthy beliefs, I will help you to come to some new, healthier conclusions. This helps you to be at peace when thinking about past events, and can also help your body heal, be emotionally liberating and help you make positive changes to your life.

Sneak Preview/Overview Of What's Coming

My intention with the Mind Detox Method is to simplify therapy and speed up self-healing.

Before we get started, I want to give you a sneak preview/overview of why the Mind Detox Method works, so that you know right from the start how simple yet profound this method can be.

Heal the Hidden Cause of Feeling Bad
Feeling bad about things in your life means that your mind believes it is justified in feeling bad in light of whatever happened. To help you to feel better, the Mind Detox Method (MDM) heals the justifications for feeling bad that are hidden in your mind. By installing positive perspectives instead, you will feel naturally more at peace with the past, present and future.

Heal the Hidden Cause of Bad Health
Chronic stress is widely regarded as being just about the main cause of physical health problems and conditions. Perhaps surprisingly, stress is not ultimately caused by external people or situations, but instead by your own inner resistance to life. The Mind Detox Method finds the hidden justifications that are causing resistance and helps you to accept life more. Your body is always healing as best it can, so as your resistance reduces, so does harmful stress, allowing the body to heal more speedily.

Heal the Hidden Cause of Bad Life Events
In a very innocent way, your mind wants to prove your beliefs right. If you have any unhealthy beliefs relating to your ability to create the life results you want, then your mind will do everything it can to make your unhealthy beliefs a living reality in your life. Put bluntly, if you believe that it is hard to make money then your mind will help you to prove that it's hard to make money! The Mind Detox Method finds the source of your unhealthy beliefs and helps you to come to more positive and productive conclusions about

yourself, other people and the world you live in. Your mind then goes to its natural work, now proving your new beliefs right rather than your old ones, and life success become easier.

The Possibilities are Infinite!

Due to the indisputable fact that your beliefs impact on your body (because of the mind–body connection), your emotions (because they justify how you feel in any given moment) and your life (because they determine your levels of success), healing unhealthy beliefs can lead to big benefits. You no longer need to be a victim of your past, and you can be free to choose a life lived with true health, wealth and happiness.

Are you excited to learn the Mind Detox Method? I promise to teach it to you soon, but first I need you to get into the optimal mindset for making genuine and long-lasting changes to your body and your life.

PART ONE

The Healing Mindset

GET READY FOR REMARKABLE RESULTS

CHAPTER ONE

Self-Healing Success Stories

. . . .

CULTIVATE THE RIGHT MINDSET
FOR CHANGING YOUR BODY AND LIFE

MIRACLES *DO* HAPPEN! I've been lucky enough to witness people from around the world heal a wide variety of physical, emotional and life problems that more conventional thinking would suggest were impossible to cure. On top of that, I've also been encouraged to see the amazing results attained by the Mind Detox Method (MDM) Practitioners whom I've had the privilege to train via my academy. This especially excites me because it shows that the MDM is a transferable skill that anyone willing to move on from past limitations can learn and benefit from.

Over the past few years, people experiencing the methods shared in this book have reported improvements with the following problems: acid reflux, acne, addictions, allergies, anxiety, asthma, arthritis, back problems, chronic pain, constipation, depression, diabetes, eating disorders, eczema, fatigue, food intolerances, headaches, hearing loss, hyperhydrosis, insomnia, irritable bowel syndrome, low self-esteem, M.E., migraines, money issues, panic attacks, psoriasis, phobias, relationship difficulties, thyroid problems, weight gain and more.

Although no guarantees can be made with regards to physical

healing, if you are experiencing ill health then I have found it to be very helpful to take a holistic approach.

Cultivate Confidence in the Mind Detox Method

To increase your confidence in what you are about to learn, please read through the real-life self-healing success stories presented in the following pages. Not only do they make for highly inspirational reading they can also help you to develop the belief that self-healing is not only possible, but inevitable, which is paramount for activating your body's inbuilt self-healing capabilities. On top of that, they can help to illustrate how changing your mind can change your life circumstances.

BENEFIT NO.1 Pain Free Without Painkillers

The body can speak the mind. If something causes you emotional pain, then it can eventually lead to physical pain. I've seen chronic pain vanish instantly when a person finds peace with their past.

• • •

Meet John, who had back pain:

> "Ever since a car accident over two years ago I had been suffering from a painful lower back. After a conversation with Sandy we discovered the root cause of why my back was vulnerable in the first place, which linked back to when my dad went into hospital for a few weeks when I was a child. When I resolved it, the pain went away immediately. That night I slept through with no painkillers (for the first time in over two years) and got up the next morning and did yoga!"

• • •

Meet Gail, who had painful knees:

> "I had been suffering with very painful and swollen knees
> for many months, so I met up with Sandy to receive a
> Mind Detox consultation. I was amazed by the results.
> The pain eased immediately, and by the following day the
> swelling had gone down and I was able to wear my beloved
> three-inch heels again. I am still pain-free and trotting
> around in my heels. Mind Detox is fantastic."

• • •

Meet Kate, who also had knee problems:

> "After a kneecap dislocation, I found myself experiencing
> extreme pain every time I tried to move my knee, making
> physiotherapy, and therefore recovery, impossible.
>
> Through working with a pain specialist physiotherapist
> I came to realize that my knee did not actually physically
> hurt at all, but that there was a psychological reason for
> the pain I was feeling. I had a session with Sandy where
> he quickly identified that the original dislocation had
> reminded me of a traumatic event from my childhood and
> the memory was manifesting itself as pain in my knee.
>
> After only one session I returned to physiotherapy and
> was able to get on an exercise bike. I regained the ability
> to walk soon after. I truly believe that if I had undergone
> traditional therapy, probably coupled with the antidepres-
> sants my doctor had been recommending, it would have
> taken many months before I recovered. Sandy's method
> is good at drawing out deeply suppressed feelings and

dissolving them. I felt euphoric after my session, like a huge weight had been lifted from my head. I would recommend Mind Detox to anyone suffering from a physical condition that won't heal."

• • •

Meet Debbie, who had period pains:

"I had been suffering from period pains for 30 years, ever since I'd started my menstrual cycle at age 13. I experienced Sandy's method when I was 43 and wish I hadn't waited so long! Every month I was left with no energy and felt out of control and resentful. I discovered during my Mind Detox consultation that I had had my first period on my 13th birthday and it made me feel dirty, uncomfortable, sad, scared and unloved. This emotionally linked with an earlier event when, aged four, I had felt the same in relation to whether my dad loved me. When I recognized that he had loved me my whole life, all the other negative emotions cleared instantly. Two weeks later I had my first pain-free period in 30 years!"

TOP TIP **Saying the Unsayable**

One way to curb chronic pain is to heal events in your life when you've not been able to speak your mind or feel your feelings. By saying the *unsayable* and feeling the *unfeelable* once and for all – in relation to people or events in your past – stored emotional stress can be released, along with physical pain.

BENEFIT NO.2 **Loving the Skin You're In**

Skin can be one of the first physical signs of a person having un-resolved emotional issues below the surface. The nature of the skin condition is often symbolic; by which I mean that skin hypersensi-tivity in the form of, for example, eczema can be the result of sepa-ration anxiety (whereby the skin is increasing its ability to "reach out and touch/find" the lost person, place, event or thing). Psoria-sis, where the skin is producing extra cells, is often the result of an external attack, such as bullying or near-death experience, which causes the body to produce an extra-thick line of defence against the perceived threat.

As the human body grows a new skin by regenerating all its skin cells every month or so, healing can occur very quickly once the reason for the skin condition is resolved.

• • •

Meet Melissa, who had eczema:

> "I was a complete self-diagnosed stress-head until I met
> Sandy. I can confidently say that I am a much more relaxed
> person now and a number of the negative health side-
> effects of the stress have completely disappeared. I also
> benefited from the drastically improved appearance of
> my skin when I resolved the Root-Cause Reason for my
> eczema (which stemmed back to an event that happened
> when I was a child). Thanks very much. I feel brilliant!"

BENEFIT NO. 3 **Brilliantly Working Bowels!**

The brain and bowels are very much emotionally connected. Similarly to the skin, the bowels are prone to speaking the mind in rather symbolic ways. For instance, people finding certain events in their life "hard to digest" can suffer with digestive problems. Those experiencing excessive stress or anxiety often end up with the additional concern of needing to find toilets quickly due to their chronic diarrhoea. People who have suffered loss in their life and experience difficulties letting go are often more likely to become constipated as their bowels stop letting go too.

Making peace with the past by using the methods in this book can help on all three counts, allowing for better functioning bowels.

• • •

Meet Tracey, who was constipated:

> "I was totally stressed out, overweight, constipated, had odema in my legs so bad that I couldn't kneel down, had no self-confidence, and sweated uncontrollably if anyone spoke to me. I am now much more confident, 12 pounds lighter, with no odema, no constipation and no sweating! Sandy's method is fantastic, and I can only thank you from the bottom of my heart – I am a new woman!"

• • •

Meet Ian, who was also constipated:

> "I had suffered from badly working bowels ever since I was a child. I worked with Sandy when I was 34 and discovered that I had a hidden belief that it wasn't safe to go to the toilet. To be honest, once we healed that out-of-date

belief I immediately had to go to the toilet as my constipation had ceased to exist! One month on and my bowels
are functioning brilliantly, and I've even lost about a stone
(6.4kgs) in weight, without dieting, now my body knows
it's safe to let go!"

BENEFIT NO. 4 **Life-Changing Weight Loss**

Excess weight is often a symptom of one or more physical and/
or emotional problem(s). Enjoying a healthy weight requires you
to explore the reasons why your body has felt the need to adapt
by gaining weight, then be willing to make a few changes to the
physical and emotional conditions in which your body exists. Doing so can cause your body to adapt again naturally, but this time
by losing weight.

• • •

Meet Susan who struggled with her weight:

"I had gained weight in my twenties, but didn't understand
why. Whatever I did to lose it didn't make much difference.
When working with Sandy I found a connection between
when the weight gain happened and what had been going
on in my life at the time. It became clear to me that the
extra weight was my body's way of protecting me from the
conflict that was happening in my family. When I let go
of the unresolved emotions relating to the difficult time in
my life, I immediately began to lose weight. It was magic!"

BENEFIT NO.5 **No Sweat!**

My method has been used to successfully treat excessive sweating, which is often linked with anxiety and anger. In the majority of cases, the Root-Cause Event is a time when lots of attention was on the person and they didn't know what to do. This caused a shock, which the body has remembered and which is why it continues to go into panic mode whenever similar events happen again. It is also common for the perspiring person to have felt unfairly treated, causing an undercurrent of anger.

• • •

Meet Alistair, who sweated excessively:

> "Despite being a very fit and healthy Royal Marine, I had
> to hide the fact that I sweated uncontrollably. I had to
> always wear dark-coloured clothes, sleep on a towel and
> couldn't go for the promotion I wanted because sweating
> was seen as a sign of being unfit. Sandy helped me get
> to parts of my mind I didn't know existed. We found a
> memory of a time at school when a teacher shouted at me
> unfairly and I felt angry that I was made to look stupid.
> When I achieved peace with the past event the excessive
> sweating that I'd had for years calmed down. I am now in
> control of the condition and able to get on with my life
> with greater confidence and peace of mind."

BENEFIT NO.6 **No More Migraines**

• • •

Meet Sophie, who had migraines:

> "For years I had suffered with debilitating migraines. Working with Sandy helped me to find what had been 'on my mind' (albeit my unconscious mind!) the entire time. I was able to change the beliefs that were causing me to feel so negative towards myself, and clear the blocks that had been preventing me from making necessary changes to the way I'd been living life.
>
> I've not had a single migraine or headache since. My relationships with my friends have improved, and my fears around having a family of my own have disappeared. I'm now very happily married, and we are even expecting our first baby. Truly life-changing!"

• • •

Meet Rachel, who also had migraines:

> "I had been suffering from regular migraines for years. During my consultation with Sandy I discovered and healed the emotional cause of the migraines, which stemmed back to when a friend committed suicide. This also linked to an earlier event when a family member died suddenly. Amazingly, my headache went away immediately when I gave myself permission to be at peace with the passing of those I love. I've not had a migraine since."

BENEFIT NO.7 **A Sweeter Life, Naturally**

I nearly fell of my chair when I heard about this success story from a Mind Detox Method (MDM) practitioner working in Mexico:

• • •

Meet Rosa, who had diabetes:

> "I had severe diabetes and my blood count was 300 [un-healthily high]. The day after my Mind Detox consulta-tion my blood count had dropped to 160! And now, three months after the consultation, my doctor has completely taken me off the medication."

BENEFIT NO.8 **Bad Behaviours, Be Gone**

Destructive behaviours such as phobias, addictions and compulsive disorders can be a thing of the past if you use the methods outlined in this book. This is mainly because your beliefs determine your emotions and your emotions drive your behaviours. By changing your emotionally fuelled beliefs, you can more easily and naturally behave however you want.

• • •

Meet Juliet, who was a compulsive cleaner:

> "Everything had to be immaculate. I was missing out on going for walks and playing outside with my child because I couldn't stand dirt. Working with Sandy I discovered that I had made an unconscious connection between dirt and feelings of vulnerability. This meant any time I saw anything unclean I would immediately feel vulnerable and need to either clean it or run away from it. When

I resolved the cause for this unconscious connection I immediately became able to enjoy being around mud and all things messy! This has freed me up to enjoy family life more, which even includes the occasional pottery lesson!"

• • •

Meet Liz, who couldn't travel abroad:

"I had not been abroad on holiday for 20 years because I got really ill on the return flight from my last holiday and was convinced the same thing was going to happen again.

A few weeks before my holiday I spent a couple of hours with Sandy, and he helped me discover the real reasons why I was so frightened about getting ill when travelling. This not only helped me to enjoy the weeks leading up to my holidays without worry but also let me enjoy the flight without being ill and without having to take medication.

I now fly abroad and within the UK quite frequently and without incident and thoroughly enjoy it. My whole life has changed, as I use the techniques Sandy gave me whenever I feel stressed and it works. I can't emphasize enough how beneficial it would be to anyone with any kind of issues, be they mental or physical, to spend some time with Sandy – it can change your life for ever."

BENEFIT NO. 9 **Cool, Calm and Confident**

I bet you are much more confident than you think! Are you confident making a cup of tea, cleaning the house or doing a hobby you love? Of course you are. This is because confidence is context-dependent. In other words, there is no such thing as "unconfident people", only those who experience habitual negative thoughts and emotions when faced with certain life events. Confidence is the natural way you feel when you are NOT thinking and feeling negatively.

People with low confidence often worry about what other people think about them. So the antidote to low confidence involves learning to love yourself more fully so you don't *need* to be liked by others.

• • •

Meet Annette, who had low self-esteem:

> "I had so many issues to sort out that if I'd just got rid of one it would have been a bonus. I have found out, using Sandy's method, that by getting to the root cause, all the related problems tumble away – and it works. It is magic. I used to think that I wasn't good enough, that everyone I love leaves me etc but now, for the very first time in my whole life, I KNOW I AM PERFECT!"

BENEFIT NO.10 Peace for Life!

The unhealthy beliefs associated with unresolved emotional events can put the body–mind into a perpetual state of stress (known as the fight-or-flight response). This can make a person more inclined to constantly search their environment for potential threats, overthink and experience chronic anxiety.

• • •

Meet Jill, who had debilitating anxiety:

> "I was getting daily bouts of anxiety. These were debilitating and stopped me doing ordinary everyday things. I would shake, feel sick, overeat to stop the nausea and rush about like a headless chicken, not really getting anywhere. Since using the methods taught by Sandy I have not had any anxiety, have much more energy, been more focused and got more done. My life, and consequently the lives of those around me, has become calmer and happier. I laugh a lot more, and I'm sleeping better. Old behaviour patterns and past traumas are now a thing of the past, as I learn to live in and enjoy each moment."

Having read these success stories, you are probably becoming increasingly excited about learning and using the same techniques that have helped these happy people enjoy such great benefits. I promise I will share the actual methods with you soon but, before I do, I want to let you in on a few secrets that sit at the heart of many of these miraculous success stories…

CHAPTER TWO

Seven Self-Healing Secrets

· · · ·

HOW THE MIND CAN HELP YOU HEAL

KNOWING THE FOLLOWING SELF-HEALING SECRETS CAN HELP YOU TO ACCESS YOUR OWN SELF-HEALING CAPABILITIES. The secrets, (called "secrets" because few people know them), explain why physical problems don't necessarily have purely physical causes, how your emotional well-being and your physical wellness are inextricably linked and why it is possible to heal your body and your life by changing your mind.

Working in accordance with these self-healing secrets has been instrumental in helping me to develop the right mindset for helping others. I believe they can help you to take control of your physical and emotional destiny, be free from chronic stress and enjoy a more fulfilling life. Ready to learn the first secret? Let's begin!

SECRET NO.1 Your Body *Is* Your Mind

What your mind believes, perceives and experiences has the potential to be sent to your entire body and cause physical responses.

A commonly held misconception in the western world is that the mind and body are separate entities: that there are physical problems and then there are mental or emotional problems. However, the mind and body is very much one entity. Mental stress and unresolved emotional unease has the potential to impact on many aspects of the physical body, and often shows up as physical conditions.

The mind–body connection has been known about for centuries, but it is only in recent years that so many scientific studies have been able to prove how thoughts and emotions affect the body:

IF YOU'RE GRATEFUL…

then you almost double certain aspects of your immune system, heal more quickly due to higher oxygenation of the tissues and positively impact the "coherence" of your heart rhythms, which can have a positive knock-on effect with many of the other essential organs too.

IF YOU'RE ANGRY…

then researchers at Ohio State University found you get a surge in cytokines, the immune molecules that trigger inflammation. High levels of cytokines are linked with arthritis, diabetes, heart disease and cancer.

IF YOU'RE JEALOUS…

then your body ends up suffering from increased blood pressure, heart rate, adrenalin levels and a weakened immunity.

IF YOU'RE IN LOVE…

then you increase the levels of nerve-growth factor, according to research at the University of Pavia in Italy. Enhanced nerve growth helps restore the nervous system and improves memory. Love has also been linked with pain relief, healthier hearts and living longer.

IF YOU'RE STRESSED OUT...

then a harmful concoction of stress hormones, including adrenalin and norepinephrine, can end up circulating through your body. Over time, stress hormones like these have been found to compromise the immune system, weaken organs, cause the body to turn off long-term building-and-repair projects, speed up the aging process and make the body more prone to developing chronic illness.

And the list goes on and on...

Your mind is linked with your autonomic nervous system (ANS), which regulates your heartbeat, blood pressure, digestion and metabolism, along with many more of the "automatic" bodily functions. Obvious autonomic mind–body connection responses include getting a red face when embarrassed, your mouth watering when you think of a food you love and experiencing butterflies in your stomach when you're feeling nervous or excited. Even sexual arousal requires the mind and body to communicate! Although we generally take these common physical reactions for granted, it's useful to take a moment to appreciate what's actually happening.

Your embarrassed red face requires thousands of chemical reactions to take place within your body along with the diversion of blood flow to your skin. That sensation of nervousness in your stomach is the blood draining from the stomach lining as it heads to the outer regions of the body to help you resist or run from the perceived external threat. When it comes to sexual arousal – well, we all know that a range of physical responses can happen if certain thoughts occur!

Chemical Messengers of the Mind

Many of these examples of the mind–body connection are known due to evidence of the mind being found to exist in the cells of your body. Neuropeptides (also known as "the molecules of emotion") are released into your bloodstream, which in turn can affect the functioning of your entire body by communicating with your individual cells.

Now there are very few places on your body that you can cut yourself where you wouldn't bleed. Similarly, there are few places in your body where you don't find neuropeptides. The body is literally riddled with the chemical messengers of your thoughts; so much so that it is scientifically accurate to say the state of your body is quite literally a physical manifestation of your mind.

Yes, that's right. Your body is a physical manifestation of your mind.

Stop to consider all the physical reactions that happen as a result of what's happening in your thoughts and emotions, and you can't help but begin to question whether your chronic back pain, skin condition or digestive disorder is the result of a purely physical phenomenon. The implications of the mind–body connection are massive when it comes to understanding why people end up with physical problems. This is especially so when you explore the extent to which your beliefs are not only known by the cells of your body but are also constantly actually causing physical changes to occur. More about this soon, but first…

LET'S PLAY A GAME

Monitoring the Mind–Body

For the next 24 hours, be highly vigilant about the physical reactions that occur in your body when you're thinking about different things, or when you're experiencing different situations. Notice what happens within your body when you:

- Think about certain memories;
- Think about someone you dislike compared to someone you love dearly;
- Think about different future scenarios that you are excited about compared to ones you're worried about;
- Find something funny and laugh;
- Find something sad and cry;
- Criticize someone/something;
- Praise and appreciate someone/something;
- Experience different external situations – like being stuck in traffic, being hugged or watching a movie.

A Vital First Step in Self-Healing

The first step in intentionally self-healing (I say intentionally, because you are unintentionally self-healing all the time!) is to notice first-hand, in your own personal life experience, that your thoughts and emotions *are* impacting on your body.

Becoming aware of this means you move from being oblivious to the ongoing, behind-the-scenes impact of the mind–body connection to a simple appreciation that it is happening. Although it may sound like a simple step, believe it or not this is a massive leap towards taking charge of your physical destiny.

When you fully appreciate that your thoughts and emotions impact upon what happens within your body, you naturally find yourself in a far better position to actively influence your physical health and well-being.

SECRET NO.2 Your Beliefs Become Your Body

Unhealthy beliefs can manifest physically as an unhealthy body.

The Biological Impact of Your Beliefs

Beliefs can impact biology due to the interconnection of the mind and body. Your beliefs are the conclusions that you've come to throughout your life about your body, your personality, your capabilities, self-worth, loveability, safety and so on.

Beliefs have been found to have the power to influence many aspects of a person's physical functioning, including digestion, immune system, blood pressure and even DNA.

The impacts of the belief–body connection range from everyday physical responses to more life-threatening results; in a very real way, your beliefs become your biology. Recognizing the impact of your beliefs can help you to increase confidence in your own self-healing capabilities.

The Miracle in Your Mouth

When you think about a food you like your body gets ready to eat it. Your salivary glands immediately go to work producing a fluid composed of water, mucus, proteins, mineral salts and amylase, an enzyme that breaks down starches.

Incredibly, your body can react differently towards foods you like and to foods you dislike. When you think about a food you don't like your body produces less saliva, making it more difficult to swallow the food you *believe* you don't like. Two very different physical responses, yet the only way the body knows to respond differently is via the beliefs you have about the different foods. Amazing!

Clockwork Orange

Perhaps even more amazing are the experiences of some people with multiple-personality disorders. There are documented cases of the same person having different physical conditions depending on which personality is prominent at any given time. In a particular case, one personality was highly allergic to oranges and the other could eat them with no allergic reaction whatsoever. In another case, one personality needed glasses to see, whereas the other had perfect 20-20 vision. In both cases, the *cause* of the differences between the personalities existed in the mind, not the body.

Placebo Power

More evidence of how beliefs impact the body is the global phenomenon of the placebo effect. The placebo effect happens when, for example, a person takes a fake pill believing it is the *real* pill, but ends up getting better anyway. In the thousands of documented cases worldwide, it is clearly the person's belief that the fake pill will work, not the ingredients of the pill, that causes healing to occur.

Just as powerful though is the harmful effect of the nocebo. The nocebo effect is the opposite of the placebo, whereby a person's beliefs play a role in them getting sick and, in some cases, even dying.

Catching a Cold

I used to get ill a couple of times every winter, when I would "catch a cold". Then one day I discovered some compelling evidence that proved to me (my mind) that it was impossible to catch a cold and, guess what, I have never caught one since. Is this a coincidence? I don't believe so.

The Clock is Ticking

Or have you ever heard about people being told that they only have a finite time to live, say three months, and they've ended up dying three months to the day of the terminal diagnosis? Is this a coincidence? Again, I don't believe so. In these common examples, I believe it is beliefs becoming the body.

Having worked with hundreds of people to help them to change beliefs, I've discovered two types of unhealthy beliefs that impact the body:

Body Beliefs and Stress Beliefs: Body beliefs relate directly to the physical functioning of the body. They are conclusions you've come to about your body that eventually become self-fulfilling prophecies, such as, *I always get the flu in winter,* or another common one: *I will gain weight with age.*

This One Actually Caught Me Out

Growing up I was constantly told that I could eat whatever I wanted but when I hit 30 years old I would need to be careful because I would get fat. Amazingly, within weeks of turning 30 I began gaining weight despite my diet and exercise regime being the same as it had always been. After a while I realized I must have picked up a body belief about gaining weight with age. So I set about doing everything I could to change not my body, but my mind.

To help disprove the unhealthy body belief I gave myself the goal of noticing all the people in my life who were older than 30 who had *not* gained weight. This helped me to naturally heal the unhealthy belief because my mind now had lots of evidence to prove that it is possible, indeed normal, to maintain a slim body the older I get. Within a few weeks my body was back to my normal weight and I could continue enjoying freedom with food.

Beliefs Stressing the Body Out of Balance

The other type of beliefs I observe in people suffering from physical conditions is what I call stress beliefs. These are the kind of beliefs that cause people to experience high levels of stress, unease and angst during daily life.

I'm not safe, I'm bad, It's my fault, I'm not good enough, or I'm abandoned are just a few examples. Amongst other unhealthy side-effects, beliefs like these can cause your mind to constantly search your life for potential threats, leading to your body being in a perpetual state of fight-or-flight survival mode and creating the increased likelihood of physical problems.

• • •

Meet Ros, who had abdominal pain:

> "I had been sent from one hospital department to the other over several years, but no one seemed to be able to discover the cause of my abdominal pain until I saw Sandy. He helped me to get to the real emotional root of the problem, and the pain that had given me years of agony disappeared. All the other associated physical and emotional problems disappeared as well. Initially I was half waiting for them to return, but two years on I'm still feeling great!"

Ros is a perfect example of how quickly the body can heal when you change unhealthy beliefs. Her hidden belief was that she was *abandoned*. We discovered that she had formed that belief aged four, when she had managed to escape from her nursery and run home only to find an empty house. Her belief that she'd been abandoned was causing her intense negative emotions, which were stressful on her body and manifesting as chronic physical pain.

*By changing your beliefs you can cause changes to occur
within your body.*

Now, the truth is, she wasn't abandoned; in fact, *she'd* run away
from nursery without telling anyone! But her belief that she was
abandoned was enough to negatively impact her health for years!
When she found peace with her past by remembering that her
mum had come home a few minutes later and she wasn't abandoned but rather had actually run away, the negative emotion
cleared, along with the physical pain.

TOP TIP **Befriend your Beliefs**

Your mind wants to prove your beliefs right. So if, for example, you
have a belief that you are abandoned, then your mind will do everything it can to help you be abandoned again and again! If you
believe life is hard then life *will* be difficult. Or if you have the belief that you aren't safe, then your mind will help you find evidence
that proves you're in danger. Not because your mind is against you;
quite the opposite – it's trying to help you be right!

Heal the Hidden Cause can help you to discover and resolve any
unhealthy beliefs that may be counterproductive to your health,
wealth and happiness. Harnessing your self-healing capabilities
requires you to befriend your beliefs by making sure they are working in your best interest.

To discover beliefs that may be impacting upon your body, it is
very useful to begin to see the symbolic way that your body speaks
your mind. Because as you do, you can discover that...

SECRET NO. 3 Your Body is Not Against You

*Symptoms most people consider to be physical problems
can in fact be your body's best attempt at staying alive.*

Survival is the primary goal of the human body. It is not designed
to just break, malfunction or get "sick" *without good reason*. Instead
it is constantly doing everything in its power to adapt to, and survive, the inner and outer conditions it is experiencing during daily
life. This happens because your body follows the orders given to it
by your mind. More specifically, the individual cells that make up
your body are so intelligent they are constantly adjusting themselves to the environment in which they *think* they exist.

Adapting to the Chemical Climate

It works like this: your mind interprets whatever is happening in the external environment and then your brain re-
leases chemical messengers of your thoughts (neuropeptides)
into the blood, which tell the cells what adjustments they
need to make in order to best survive the perceived environment. So, in the same way you would adapt to a change in the
weather when it rains by putting a rain jacket on, your individual cells adapt to their chemical climate and the different
chemical messengers they are flooded with on a daily basis.
Your mind–body is communicating this way now. The millions of
cells that make up your body are listening to your mind and re-
sponding accordingly. This means that if you are, for example, being loving, your heart is quite literally experiencing love. If you feel
unsupported, your knees feel it physically. Or if you're feeling fear,
your entire body is on physical red alert, with the fight-or-flight
response working overtime. Physical symptoms are often highly

symbolic of issues at the mind level; the body does a brilliant job of speaking the mind.

Cast Your Mind Back

Remember Alistair, who had excessive sweating? We discovered during our consultations that his sweat was, in his words, "anger bubbling up inside". When he let go of the pent-up anger, his body stopped the excessive sweating. Or Ian, whose constipation was the result of his body believing it wasn't safe to go to the toilet after an "accident" as a child. His body was trying to help him by becoming constipated! Other examples that spring to mind include:

• • •

Anna, who had psoriasis:

> "My legs had been completely covered with psoriasis for over 25 years. I discovered, using Sandy's method, that it was my body's way of protecting me from a series of external threats, including bullying, that I had encountered during my teenage years. Within a few weeks of healing the fears associated with the past bullying, the skin on my legs was back to normal."

• • •

Meet Julie, who had lost her hearing:

> "About 18 months ago I was diagnosed with Meniere's disease, a condition which affects the inner ear with excess fluid build-up, leading to debilitating attacks of severe vertigo, vomiting, tinnitus and eventually damage to the hearing, often causing permanent hearing loss. Gradually

my hearing in my right ear had deteriorated to the point of fluctuating between severe loss and moderate loss. I had needed to resort to getting a hearing aid fitted.

I attended the Mind Detox Method Practitioner training with Sandy in Australia. During the course Sandy demonstrated a one-on-one session with me in which I discovered a memory of my parents divorcing when I was six. I was scared at the time about not knowing what was going to happen, and I felt unloved. Sandy helped me recognize that life did go on and that I was loved.

After our session I kept forgetting to wear my hearing aid. I didn't think much of it until I was doing the meditation course with Sandy the following weekend and I could clearly hear a conversation on the other side of the room. At first I doubted it, as I could not normally hear a conversation that far away, even with my hearing aid. That night, to my surprise, I put my headphones in my right ear first and found I could hear! Normally it would be muffled but this time it was loud and clear. I had my hearing back and I sense the Meniere's has gone too! So perhaps what I needed to hear the most was that I'm loved! Thank you so much, Sandy, I'm now able to hear that I'm loved and so much more. I am forever grateful."

• • •

Also, meet Sandra, who had period pains for 20 years:

"Ever since I was a teenager I had suffered from intense cramps every month. I thought it was just something I had to grin and bear … until I heard about the Mind Detox Method. We discovered an event in my past where I had lost someone I loved dearly. When I resolved the resistance to letting go of that person, I immediately felt a release in my body. I have experienced hardly any period pain since."

Sandra was resisting the loss of someone she loved and her body was resisting letting go each month – in the physical manifestation of period pains. As you can see from these real-life examples, the human body is constantly adapting to survive in light of the climate of your mind. By changing your mind for the better, your body can naturally change again, but this time by functioning in a more desirable way.

ENJOYING THIS BOOK?

Due to the body's natural tendency to respond positively to positive messages, simply reading a book like this can potentially benefit your health in miraculous ways. Amazing, isn't it!

LET'S EXPLORE Your Body Speaks Your Mind

Consider how your body may be speaking your mind through the creation of your current physical condition. Just for now, let go of any medical labels you may have been given, and instead, explore the physical condition from a fresh perspective. Very useful questions to consider are:

- What is happening within my body, i.e. what is my body actually doing?
- How might the physical conditions be an attempt to adapt, be safe and/or survive my past or current life circumstances?
- If the physical condition was trying to send a symbolic message to me, what might it be saying?

- If the physical condition was a negative emotion, what emotion would it be?
- How might my body be mirroring my life?
- Taking account of what's happened in my life, how might my body today be a physical manifestation of my past?
- What was happening in my life during the 12–18 months leading up to when I first noticed the physical condition? What bad things were happening? What good things were happening? What problematic situation was resolved?

This is an awareness-raising exercise; it gives you the opportunity to explore whether there may be any possible mind-based causes for your physical condition. If you think you've found a possible cause, then hopefully the rest of this book can help you take positive steps towards self-healing.

SECRET NO.4 Resistance is Bad for Your Health

Resisting life is the ultimate cause of almost all pain, negative emotions and harmful forms of stress.

The Result of Regular Resistance

Although short bouts of stress can actually boost immunity and raise levels of cancer-fighting molecules, being in a perpetual state of stress is a very different story. Your body ends up turning off long-term building-and-repair projects, and instead speeds up the aging process and weakens its immunity. Not only that, numerous scientific studies have also found evidence that firmly links negative emotions with the onset of arthritis, diabetes, heart disease, cancer and other problems.

According to Stanford University Medical School, the Centers for Disease Control and Prevention in Atlanta (CDC) and numerous health experts, the main cause of health problems on the planet is stress. Pointing to one very simple strategy for self-healing:

To increase health, we must reduce stress.

The Root Cause of Stress

However, in my opinion it is neither the stress nor negative emotions that are the *ultimate cause* of many physical and emotional problems. Rather, it's a person's resistance to life that is the problem. Resistance not only causes the body stress but is also highly instrumental in whether or not a person feels negative emotions.

Experiencing anger, sadness, fear, guilt or grief is only possible if you resist something in your past, present or future. Anger or sadness is usually the result of resisting something in your past, whereas resisting the possibility of something bad happening in the future usually causes fear and anxiety. Irrespective of the emotion, resistance is the underlying cause.

What makes things worse for the body is the fact that most people would prefer to not experience negative emotions, and so end up resisting not only life but their emotions too! I often see this leading to a never-ending vicious circle of a person resisting more and more day by day, putting their body under ever-increasing levels of stress. No wonder this compounded stress often ends up with people experiencing physical disease!

Fortunately, it is never life events that cause you stress or make you feel bad, but rather your resistance to what's happened/happening. Which ultimately means that you have a choice. If you can learn to let go of resistance, you can massively reduce stress and persistent negative emotions. They can be immediately replaced by feelings of inner peace, gratitude and contentment; which are, incidentally, emotions that have all been found to aid the healing process.

From Problems to Peace

Most therapy clients I meet are resisting something. If they weren't, there would be no reason for them to work with me because everything would be okay! By using the Mind Detox Method, I've helped them to find places in their lives where they've been resisting and, during the course of the consultations, have been able to help them move from a place of resistance to one of acceptance.

By finding the subtle, often well-hidden resistances in your life and moving from a place of resistance to acceptance, you can significantly reduce the amount of stress your body experiences. The less stress, the more healing can and will occur, not to mention the fact that you will feel much more peaceful, contented and happy.

But what if Something Bad is Happening?

Do you just accept it? Yes, in a manner of speaking, but "accepting" it doesn't mean you can't change it. It just means you don't cause yourself unnecessary stress and suffering while you go about changing whatever isn't acceptable to you. When you are less stressed and not experiencing negative emotions you have more inner peace, mental clarity and confidence. From that more peaceful and intuitive perspective, you become a very powerful and effective person. You are able to choose to change your circumstances; the difference if you've accepted things is that you can now make changes without having to experience any negative emotions to justify your choices or actions. You simply decide for something different to happen and welcome whatever happens next.

Life-Changing Question

So if you are currently experiencing a physical condition or know that you often find yourself feeling negative emotions such as anger, sadness, fear or loneliness, then there is a very important question you must ask yourself:

What in my life am I resisting?

Explore this question further by considering:

- Am I resisting the way I've been treated by a family member, friend or colleague?
- Am I resisting the job that I do, my bank balance, or any other aspect of my life?
- Am I resisting my physical health?
- Should certain things in my life have turned out differently?
- Do I still feel bad when I think about things that have happened in the past?
- Do I feel discontent with any areas of my life?

Answering these questions can help you to highlight the areas of your life that you might be resisting. Remember, resistance is stressful for the body and the body heals best when it rests. Resistance also causes negative emotions, so peace comes from learning to resist life less. Be super-attentive to what you might be resisting, and note what you discover in a journal so that you can rise above resistance for better health, peace of mind and happiness.

SECRET NO. 5 **Cure the Hidden Root-Cause Reasons**

The cause of your resistance usually exists in the hidden parts of your mind. This can make it hard to stop resisting life – unless you know how.

Secret No. 4 shared how resistance is often the *ultimate cause* of physical conditions. But what's important to appreciate about resistance is that it is often not intentional and is very much the result of what's going on in the more subtle, hidden parts of your mind.

Most people I meet are usually aware of the surface-level results of resistance, i.e. that they feel sad about the past, worried about the future or stressed about what's happening today; but they live unaware of the underlying reasons as to why they feel the way they do.

Shining a Light on the Hidden Mind

Tune in to your mind by noticing your thoughts. The ones you can "hear" have made their way up to your conscious awareness. They exist in what's called your conscious mind. However, there is also a level to your mind that operates below the surface of consciousness, which you are "unconscious" of.

Working tirelessly behind the scenes, your unconscious mind performs many remarkable tasks without you having to be aware of any of them. It manages your memories, creates your emotions, drives your behaviours and is instrumental in healing your body. Understanding how the unconscious mind works and, more specifically, how it impacts the degree to which you resist life and experience negative emotions, is vital when helping the body to heal.

Uncovering the Subtle Cause of Resistance

Have you ever noticed how the exact same event can happen to two different people, whether that's giving a presentation or a flight being delayed, but one person will get very upset and stressed while the other takes it in their stride? Different responses to the exact same events are possible because we all have a unique version of reality.

> *Your version of reality is the result of your unique unconscious filters.*

It works like this. You gather information about your external environment via your five senses. At the point it reaches your brain and body it is raw data, without meaning – just light reflecting off the back of your eye to create pictures and vibration, making your eardrum move to produce sound.

Your unconscious mind then takes that raw data and makes meaning from the information by drawing on your internal filters, including your language, beliefs, values, past decisions, memories, significant emotional events and a few more. This unconscious process deletes, distorts and generalizes the data to create your unique version of reality – unique because you have a unique set of internal filters. Helping your body heal by reducing stress therefore requires you to change any filters that are causing you to resist life events.

Discover the Real Root-Cause Reason

By far the most impactful filter, which has the biggest impact on health, wealth and happiness, is that of your beliefs; they work silently behind the scenes, justifying the emotions you feel as you encounter different life events. Beliefs exist in the more subtle unconscious realms of your mind, which can make them difficult to find and fix – unless you know how! To do exactly this, the method you are about to learn in Part 2 first helps you to find what I refer to as the Root-Cause Event (RCE).

This is the significant emotional event in your life when it is most likely you first created the unhealthy belief. Then, to discover what the unhealthy belief is, my method goes on to find the Root-Cause Reason (RCR), which is a short sentence that includes the emotion(s) you felt at the time and the reasons why the Root-Cause Event made you feel that way. Make sense so far? Okay, let's continue.

Discovering the Root-Cause Reason requires you to recognize that it is never *what* happened, but instead, *why* it happened, that was a problem for you; that is, the *real* problem. In other words, it is the meaning you attached to what happened, the emotions you felt as a result and the subsequent conclusions that you came to (or already had), that determine whether or not something is a problem for you.

Therefore, the Root-Cause Reason, in most cases, is a short sentence that summarizes in a few words *why* what happened was a problem for you; this usually consists of one or more negative emotions and the main reason you felt or feel that way. Examples include: *Sad, scared and vulnerable when Dad left, angry made to look stupid, rejected when Mum preferred my brother* and *scared Mum weak.*

The Emotional Domino Effect

You cannot change what happened in your past, but you can change how you relate to what happened. Therefore, to heal your past, you do NOT heal *what* happened, but instead, *why* what happened was a problem for you: in other words, the Root-Cause Reason. Even better news is that if you focus on healing the Root-Cause Reasons justifying your unhealthy beliefs, you can heal multiple memories simultaneously.

By finding the theme that ties your problematic memories together you can heal a lifetime of emotional baggage in minutes!

Such a claim is possible due to the way the mind works. Your unconscious mind works behind the scenes, helping you to recognize the people, places, events and things you encounter during your daily life. By asking, *Where have I seen / heard / smelt / felt / tasted this before?* and then searching your memories for similar experiences, you can make more sense of whatever is happening in each moment.

To make its job easier, your mind links similar memories together. For instance, it connects memories about the same place or person. This is why when you hear a particular song it might remind you of a particular person, place or event, and before you know it you're taking a jaunt down memory lane. Or why things can be so emotionally difficult after a relationship break-up; everywhere you go and everything you experience can end up reminding you of the very person you're trying to forget!

The great news is that, because your memories are linked together, you can benefit from what I call the *emotional domino effect*. By clearing the emotion associated with one key memory, (what I call the Root-Cause Event), you can clear the emotions from all associated memories too – simultaneously! This makes it possible to clear a huge amount of emotional baggage in a very short amount of time.

The trick to the emotional domino effect is to find the common thread that ties your problematic past memories together.

Exploring the Common Themes

Explore what theme(s) link the majority of your "bad" memories together. You can do the same with your life problems too. In many cases, if you find the theme you will be well on your way to finding and healing your hidden unhealthy beliefs. For example, you may discover that you always tend to feel "lost" or "isolated", "abandoned" or "not wanted", "alone" or "not loved" or "a failure", "let down" or "lonely" or "unprotected" etc. The theme often becomes an unhealthy belief – such as "I'm lost", or "I'm not loved". Therefore, you want to focus on healing the theme of being "lost" or "unloved". I've found repeatedly that by healing the reasons *why* your problems have existed, your problems have no alternative but to disappear for good. Imagine that!

SECRET NO. 6 Unhealthy Beliefs can be Easy to Heal

The belief that it is hard to change unhealthy beliefs is a belief you can easily change!

Beliefs play a key role in determining the health of your body and the quality of your life. However, whenever I used to sit down with clients and tell them we were going to change one of their unhealthy beliefs I would commonly see the whites of their eyes! This probably had a lot to do with the myth that states that it is hard to change beliefs. In my experience this simply isn't true; we are actually forming new beliefs all the time.

What's Hiding in your Closet?

I bet there is an item of clothing in your wardrobe that you bought a few years ago that, at the time, you *believed* made you look good. You strutted your stuff and felt fantastic wearing it! However, your tastes in clothing have changed so much that now someone would need to pay *you* to wear it! Fashion tastes changing is just one example of beliefs changing easily and naturally.

Desiring to help my clients more easily change their minds, I started referring to beliefs in a way that made the idea of changing them seem more palatable. These days I often call them conclusions.

Beliefs are nothing more than conclusions you've come to at some point in your life, based upon the limited information you had available at the time.

Making sense of the world you were born into, you came to conclusions about your personality (if you're outgoing or shy), your tastes (what you like or dislike), your capabilities (what you can and can't do), your self-worth, lovability and so on. Many of these conclusions do serve you well (I'd suggest you are doing a much better job of being you than you may sometimes give yourself credit for!) However, some conclusions may be negatively impacting your health, wealth, relationships, career and life success. The good news is that, if you have come to some unhelpful conclusions, there are three reasons why they can be easy to heal:

REASON NO.1   Beliefs are not Absolutely True

Truth is always true. Beliefs are only sometimes correct, in some circumstances, for a select few, in limited locations, at certain times. Truths, on the other hand, are always true, in all circumstances, for everyone, in all time and space.

The good news is that *all* beliefs are only relatively true. Any conclusion you have, such as, "It's hard to make money", may appear correct for you, but I can guarantee that someone else on the planet believes the exact opposite. So which belief is true? Both!

But it doesn't make either belief absolutely true, only relatively true. Get the difference? Because beliefs are only relatively true, they are not fixed. Beliefs can be changed... easily!

> *You are not a victim of your belief system.*
> *You can change it if it isn't working for you – and I'd*
> *recommend that you do so if any of your beliefs are limit-*
> *ing your health, wealth, peace, love and happiness.*

REASON NO. 2   Beliefs are Fuelled by Feelings not Facts

Consider this: how do you know something is true for you? Most people say, because a) it feels true, and b) I have evidence to prove it to be true. They'd be right; however, these criteria do not make their beliefs *absolutely* true.

One reason why people believe their beliefs for so long without questioning them is because they feel true. You have many thoughts passing through your mind every day that do not limit your life or impact your body in any way. You have thoughts that feel true to you. These are your beliefs. But guess what happens when you clear the emotions associated with the unhealthy beliefs? Yes, that's right – they immediately start to feel less true. Also, you stop believing them as much.

REASON NO. 3   Beliefs are based upon Limited Information

Amazingly, you came to most of your core beliefs about yourself, other people and the world you live in by the age of six, a sprinkling more by age 12 and then only a few others since. Meaning you could have beliefs affecting your health when you're 40 that you came to when you were four! (Which is what I find with many people I meet.)

The younger you came to these conclusions the less conscious awareness and life experience you had. No wonder your unhealthy beliefs are rarely correct! The good news is that, naturally, you know much more now than you did in the past. More importantly, with new information you can come to new conclusions any time you want. I mean it! (You will find this out for yourself in Part 2)

SECRET NO.7 Being Present Helps the Body to Heal

Thankfully, to enjoy more peace we don't need to become time travellers, able to change the past or future. We just need to learn to be more present.

So far you've discovered that to help your body heal you need to stop resisting your life – past, present and future. You also need to prioritize your peace by letting go of anger, sadness, fear, guilt, grief and anxiety, along with any other downward-spiralling emotional experiences.

Sound Difficult? In Reality, It Need Not Be

Freeing yourself from resistance and negative emotions can become much easier when you know and directly experience the benefits of this final secret, which incidentally is perhaps one of the best-kept secrets in history. Namely, that *this* moment is the *only* moment that exists, and therefore, the only moment that is real. This one! No other. Not some past memory or future possibility, only now.

Unfortunately, millions of people live their entire lives not recognizing this simple truth. They go through their days going over their past or pre-playing future scenarios in their mind, again and again and again, suffering from unnecessary stress, ill health and struggle in the process, simply because they are in their heads thinking about the past and future, missing the present moment.

Your Body Doesn't Know the Difference

Numerous scientific studies have now discovered that, biochemically speaking, your body cannot tell the difference between what is happening in the real world and what is imagined in your mind. Meaning that even if you are only *thinking* about a stressful situation, your body still experiences the same negative physical reactions as it would if these events were *actually* happening in reality. Quite remarkable, I'm sure you'll agree! The implications of these findings are hugely significant when it comes to your self-healing. Not only does it explain why so many people on the planet are experiencing physical conditions, it also validates the importance of learning how to think less and be more present.

The Light Relief from Seeing the Light

Words cannot describe the relief that came to me the day I discovered that my memories from the past, irrespective of how bad or sad they were, are only accessible now via my imagination. The same went for my future fears. For years I'd quite literally been scared by my shadow, my imagination. Therapy to change or let go of my problems became so much easier once I knew that the past was nothing more than an imagined story in my mind.

Product of My Overactive Imagination

When I was a child I snuck into the television room late one evening and watched the movie *Jaws*. It scared me to death! For weeks after seeing the movie I couldn't sleep; I was convinced the big shark from the movie was hiding in my wardrobe, waiting for me to go to sleep before it came out to eat me! Now, looking back on it I can't help but laugh at the thought of a giant fish living in my wardrobe, but at the time it felt so real that I would sweat and shake from fear. When my parents tried to tell me it wasn't real, it was just my imagination, I didn't believe them because it *felt* so real. But they spoke the truth, and gave me one of the most important lessons of my life. I've now discovered that my problems exist mainly in my mind, in either my imagined past or future, rarely in the real world of *this* moment.

Although the problems that cause you emotional stress may feel real, they exist more in your imagination than in reality.

Bitter Pill?

Now I appreciate this might be a bit hard to swallow at first, especially if your problems feel real and appear to be happening now. But for the sake of your health, I invite you to notice that much of the stress and negative emotions you experience are caused by overly thinking about the past and future.

• • •

Meet Mandy, who had been negatively impacted by past events for over 20 years:

> "I came to Sandy's retreat having been troubled by negative emotions relating to three people for over 22 years. These memories had impacted my weight and I'd suffered from anger and depression. After my one-to-one with Sandy I felt unburdened, and completely relieved of all the pain I'd been carrying."

Mandy recognized during our meeting that the things she considered problems today were not problems in reality, but only stories in her mind. She let go of 22 years of pain in a matter of minutes when she realized she was causing herself unnecessary stress by continuing to think about what had happened in her past. Once I showed her how to be more present she was able to recognize the difference between being present and being in her head thinking about the past. That gave her the choice to either stay in the peace of the present moment or step into the pain of her past stories. It also stopped her being a victim to a past she couldn't change.

Move Beyond Problems, for Good

By being present you can free yourself from harmful stress as you resist life less. You will do less holding on to the past and fighting what might happen in the future as you work to develop your mind so that it becomes the (peaceful) master and the body becomes the servant; or, in other words, so that the body follows the mind.

The natural by-product of a peaceful mind is a resting body. A resting body is able to heal as it naturally wants to, enabling it to be in balance, function as it was meant to, age well and experience true vitality.

By letting go of the unhealthy beliefs and judgements held within your mind, you can experience life as if there is nothing wrong. Life is perfect. You are perfect. Life is complete. You are complete. Life isn't broken, and neither are you.

You rest in the knowledge that better health, peace of mind and happiness is your birthright, your most natural way of being. This comes to you when you stop resisting life and, instead, focus your attention on enjoying the peace that occurs naturally when you are fully embracing the present moment.

(For much more guidance on how to be present and think less about the past and future, you may want to check out my other book: *THUNK! How to Think Less for Serenity and Success* (Findhorn Press, 2012.)

SUMMARY OF THE 7
SELF-HEALING SECRETS

SECRET NO.1 **Your Body *is* Your Mind**

Evidence of the mind can be found throughout your entire body, meaning that it is scientifically accurate to say that your body is a physical manifestation of your mind. As a result, your physical wellness is very much linked with your mental and emotional well-being.

SECRET NO.2 **Your Beliefs Become Your Body**

Beliefs impact upon how you relate to your life, and therefore the stress you experience. Your beliefs also determine the messages sent between the mind and the body, which in turn can impact upon the body's physical functioning.

SECRET NO.3 **Your Body is Not Against You**

Symptoms many people consider to be physical problems are often in fact your body's best attempt at adapting to survive. By changing how you perceive life, your body can adapt again, this time by starting to function in a more desirable way.

SECRET NO.4 **Regular Resistance is Bad for Your Health**

Chronic stress, caused by chronic resistance, is a major cause of problems. By learning to resist life less, you give your body more opportunities to heal.

SECRET NO.5 **Cure the Hidden Root-Cause Reasons**

By changing your unconscious unhealthy beliefs you can help your body heal, let go of stored emotional baggage, change unhelpful behaviours and enjoy enhanced well-being.

SECRET NO. 6 **Unhealthy Beliefs Can be Easy to Heal**

It is a myth that beliefs are hard to heal. Beliefs can be changed because they are never absolutely true, are fuelled by feelings not facts and are based upon limited and often wrong information. With new insight you can come to new conclusions any time you want.

SECRET NO. 7 **Being Present Helps the Body to Heal**

Much physical stress arises from thinking about the past and future. To be present is to be beyond your mind, resting in the still conscious awareness that is your Real Self. We will look at this in more detail in Part 3. When the mind rests, the body heals. Naturally, you enjoy better health, more peace of mind and more happiness.

Now that you know my self-healing secrets you are ready to experience the method for yourself. It's time to discover any hidden unhealthy beliefs that may be negatively impacting your health and happiness, so you can be free from them – for good!

PART TWO

Discover the Hidden Cause

. . . .

DISCOVER THE UNHEALTHY BELIEFS THAT ARE CAUSING PHYSICAL, EMOTIONAL AND LIFE PROBLEMS

I HIGHLY RECOMMEND YOU...

Prepare Properly

Read chapters 3, 4, 5 and 6 before attempting to use my method on any problem. Please do not use this method on your own without the guidance of a trained Mind Detox practitioner if you believe there is a chance you could find a past event that you would not want to work on by yourself. If in doubt, please see the Clinics area of my website (*www.minddetox.com*) to find a trained and qualified practitioner near you. International consultations are also available via Skype.

No Problem?

If you have no physical, emotional and life problems right now, then read through the list of Top 20 Unhealthy Beliefs in Appendix 2 (page 153) to check that you don't have any beliefs that could cause you problems in the future. If none of these unhealthy beliefs feel true, then great! Check out the "My Conclusions" tool in the Appendix to find any beliefs that you may have that are not working for you, and use the method to find when you formed the unhelpful belief and change it, for good.

CHAPTER THREE

10 Prep Steps
Before Beginning

• • • •

FOR THE BEST RESULTS PLEASE
TAKE THESE 10 PREP STEPS

GET YOURSELF READY FOR REAL RESULTS! Equally as important as the method itself is the state that you are in when doing the work. If you attempt to do the Mind Detox Method without being in the right frame of mind, it can be tricky. To help you, here are the 10 prep steps that I encourage you to follow:

PREP STEP NO.1   Be Innocent

The chances are you've read other "health" books and this isn't your very first attempt at healing your physical condition, emotional issue or life problems. Most people who use my method have tried other approaches, and may have been let down. However, irrespective of what's happened in the past, you need to step forward with fresh eyes and an open mind and believe that this is going to work for you.

I encourage you to trust the process, suspend judgement and jump in with as much childlike curiosity and innocence as you can muster. Leave doubt at the door when using the methods outlined in this book and do your best to not let scepticism steal your success.

PREP STEP NO. 2 Be Willing to Change

Although, in reality, most people's comfort zones are pretty uncomfortable, self-limiting beliefs, health problems and challenging life circumstances can become familiar. And with familiarity, there can come a sense of security. Be completely honest with yourself when considering these questions:

- Are you willing to draw a line in the sand and step out into perhaps unfamiliar territory?
- Are you willing to do things differently?
- Are you willing to trust the process, even if at the start, some parts may seem pointless?
- Are you willing to do whatever it takes to build momentum towards new healthier habits?

If the answer to all of these is "yes", then you are reading the right book.

PREP STEP NO. 3 Be Beyond Your Story

Sometimes we can be so close to our life that we can't see the wood for the trees. Or, in other words, we can get so lost in our personal story that we don't actually know what we need to work on. At the beginning of every Mind Detox consultation I allow time and space for my clients to share their story of what they see as the wrongs and rights of whatever is happening in their life. But – without wanting to sound rude – I don't actually listen to the story! Instead, I listen beyond the words so that I am better able to offer clarity on what we actually need to work. To do this I remember…

> *In life, you either get the results you want or the reasons why you're not getting what you want.*

Mind Detox works to clear the reasons why you haven't been getting the results you want. Reasons usually include ill health, negative emotions and unhelpful habits. With this in mind, consider this: What do you want to let go of? Do you want to:

- Heal a physical condition
- Clear emotional baggage (including anger, sadness, fear, guilt, hurt, grief and anxiety)
- Stop creating a negative life situation?
- Is there anything else specific you want to work on?

Note your reasons under these main categories now.

PREP STEP NO. 4 Be Clear on the Results You Want

For you to get the results you want, it is vital that you begin with a clear positive intention. Again, to keep things simple, you can categorise your results under two main headings: states and outcomes. States that you may want to focus on creating are:

- happiness
- peace
- love
- confidence
- contentment

The great news with states is that the ingredients for any state you want are already residing within you, which means that it need not take much time to enjoy the states you want. (Keep reading to discover my top tips on cultivating states.). Outcomes, on the other hand, can sometimes take time to create. Do you want to meet a loving life partner, start your own business or be slimmer? When considering the outcomes you want, it is very important that you are super-clear on how you will know when you've achieved your goal. Doing this will give you a fixed future moment when you will know that the work is done.

PREP STEP NO.5 Be Easy On Yourself

Reading a book like this one can make you more aware of how your thoughts, emotions and lifestyle might be negatively impacting on your physical health. But what's very important to keep in mind is that, although your health, wealth and happiness – or lack of them – are your responsibility, you have not intentionally done it to yourself and it is not your fault. The ultimate cause of your thinking patterns, emotional habits and behaviours exists in the more subtle realms of your mind; therefore, blaming yourself or feeling guilty about what's happening to your body or life does not help you to heal. Quite the opposite, in fact. Be easy on yourself and gently make whatever positive changes you can, at a pace that is comfortable for you.

PREP STEP NO.6 Be the Genius You Already Are

You may not think it but you are an absolute genius! Whenever I sit in front of clients at my Mind Detox clinics or retreats I make sure that I look to see the genius within. I assume that every person I meet knows the answers to every question I'm going to ask them (especially when they think they don't!) and fully expect them to be able to make any change that is required of them.

The magical thing is that when I see the genius in others, they begin to see it within themselves. There is no doubt in *my* mind that you can do it; you should think the same of yourself.

PREP STEP NO. 7 **Be a Miracle-Maker**

All things are possible. I'm not sure where I picked up this belief, but I have noticed that it is a key ingredient to doing the work covered in this book. Without living with the possibility that all things are possible, I would have probably turned away 95 per cent of the people I've successfully worked with. I would have never attempted to help the first person who walked through my door with a skin condition or digestive disorder, or was convinced that they were depressed. I would have bought in to the limiting belief that these were physical conditions and mind-based therapeutic work could not help.

Thankfully, my open-mindedness to the possibility that all things are possible gave me permission to "give it a go" and see what happened. I invite you now to trust your miraculous body and the wise universe to take care of the details. Your job is simply to be open to the possibility and proceed with optimism.

PREP STEP NO. 8 **Be Committed**

Do you really want to heal and/or experience life differently? Are you willing to persist until you get the results you want? People who have had complete remissions from illnesses or transformed their life for the better have made it their number one priority, for as long as it has taken. Commitment makes the realization of your desired results inevitable because instead of focusing on whether you will do it, you focus your attention on why you want it and what you can actively do to get it. I certainly didn't do it in a day, and I continue to practise the techniques shared here. Decide now to do what it takes to succeed!

PREP STEP NO. 9   Be One-Pointed

There is an old Chinese proverb:

> *Man who tries to cross a river in more than one boat is bound to find himself getting wet.*

I love this quote because it summarizes so perfectly the importance of being one-pointed. One-pointedness essentially means taking action without being tentative, and your mind, body and the universe respond quickest if you proceed in this way. In my experience, Mind Detox works if you don't give up too soon. Don't try it to see if it works; instead, do it until it does. You might find that your issue is resolved with the first Mind Detox you do, or you might need to find and heal a few unhealthy beliefs to get the results you want. Either way, by being one-pointed in your actions you can massively improve your chances of success.

PREP STEP NO. 10   Be Here Now

Finally, and perhaps most important to remember and practise, is to be here now. I recommend that immediately before you begin using the Mind Detox Method you become as present as possible. Clear your mind from what's been happening today and give the task at hand your fullest attention.

When you are engaged in thinking, your focus is on the past and future. Depending on what you are thinking about, you can inadvertently end up using your sympathetic nervous system, being in fight-or-flight mode and operating from your brainstem. The primary objective of this part of your brain is survival, and as a result you can become very black and white in your thinking and close yourself off to more creative and conscious ways of viewing life. This is, obviously, not the best state to be in when doing this kind of work on change.

Your body–mind will do better if you are operating more from your parasympathetic nervous system; this will make it easier to access the answers you need to move through the Mind Detox Method easily and effectively. By doing so you will enter what's often referred to as the "waking state of trance". You will find that you have fewer thoughts, your intuition is more easily accessed and change is effortless. Entering this supreme state means that you are harnessing the power of your mind–body connection.

Among other things, this amazing connection makes you physically wired to feel certain ways when you do certain things with your body. Simply putting your shoulders back, puffing your chest up and out, having a solid stance (so you are stable on your feet), breathing in a deep and balanced way and putting a big smile on your face can all help you cultivate a better state of mind. Not only that, but there is even a way of using your eyes that automatically causes you to feel calm, confident and confident – in a matter of moments.

TOP TOOL

3C Vision Instructions

In order to become present and access the ideal state of being for making changes to your mind, I recommend that you use one of my favourite tools ever: 3C Vision. This technique uses your eyes to activate your parasympathetic nervous system. It is very natural, easy and it's worked for everyone (yes, everyone!) I have ever taught. Here's how you do it:

STEP NO.1 Pick a spot on a wall to look at, ideally above eye level (at about a 45° angle), so that as you look at it, it feels as though your vision is bumping up against your eyebrows.

STEP NO. 2 As you stare at the spot on the wall, effortlessly let your mind go loose and focus all of your attention on the spot. At this point you may find yourself wanting to take a deep breath in and out. Let yourself do so.

STEP NO. 3 Notice that within a matter of a few moments, your vision will begin to spread out. You will begin to see more in the peripheral than in the central part of your vision.

STEP NO. 4 Now, pay more attention to the peripheral part of your vision than to the central part. Notice colours, shadows, shapes and so on. Notice what you see on the left and right, above and below. Be mindful that you stick to using your peripheral vision by avoiding looking directly at anything.

STEP NO. 5 Continue for as long as you want while noticing what happens. You will find that your mind is more still.

With a little practice you will be able to use 3C Vision as you go about your day – when reading, out walking, chatting with friends, pretty much any time you want to feel calm and centred and be here now. When using it in conjunction with the Mind Detox Method, simply engage 3C Vision as you progress through the method.

"If you can follow instructions, remain open-minded and trust your first answers to the questions you will be asked, you can expect to enjoy remarkable results from using the Mind Detox Method, which is outlined in the next chapter..."

CHAPTER FOUR

Discover Your Unhealthy Beliefs

• • • •

THE "DISCOVER" PART OF THE MIND DETOX METHOD

VIRTUALLY EVERY ASPECT OF YOUR DAILY LIFE IS IMPACTED BY YOUR CURRENT BELIEFS. Unhealthy beliefs have the power to impact on your body (due to the mind–body connection), your emotions (because they impact on how you interpret life) and your life circumstances (because your beliefs determine your choices and actions). Therefore, by healing your unhealthy beliefs it is possible to cause positive changes within your body, your emotions and your life.

Despite this, many people find it hard to change their unhealthy beliefs because they don't know what they are, how to find them or how to change them. Fortunately for you, this is exactly what my 5-Step Method does!

Summary of 5-Step Method

My method heals the hidden unhealthy beliefs that may be causing your current problems. To find the beliefs, we access them via a significant emotional event in the past; the event in response to which it is most likely that you formed the belief. To do this, choose a current problem you want to heal and follow these five steps:

STEP NO.1 **When Did It Start?**
Finds the age of the Root-Cause Event.

STEP NO.2 **What Happened?**
Helps you to recall the memory of what happened.

STEP NO.3 **Why Was It a Problem?**
Explores why what happened was a problem for you so you can define the Root-Cause Reason.

STEP NO.4 **Why Not a Problem Now?**
Considers what you know now to be at peace with the past.

STEP NO.5 **Test the Work**
Checks the emotional rating for how the memory feels when you think about it now. If the memory feels neutral, then the unhealthy belief is healed.

(See Appendix 1 for a key to important terms)

Ready to Heal the Hidden Cause? Let's Work Through the 5-Step Method Now

STEP NO.1 **When Did It Start?** (Find Root-Cause Event)
Choose the physical condition, emotional issue or life problem that you would like to heal. With your permission, let's find out when this problem started so that you can move on and stop it being a problem now. Trust your first answer to these questions:

> **ASK:** What event in my life is the cause of (state problem here), the first event, which when resolved will cause the problem to disappear? If I were to know, what age was I?

(For example, "What event in my life is the cause of the psoriasis/anxiety/depression/migraines, the first event which when resolved…")

TOP TIP Avoid editing your thoughts or disregarding your immediate answer if it is not what you expected. In most cases, the Root-Cause Event happened before the age of 10, so if you trust and go with your first answer you are more likely to have discovered the right Root-Cause Event.

From an initial sea of infinite possibilities, the answer to this question narrows your investigations down to a specific moment in time, like you at age two, six or 16. This will help your mind to uncover the memory of the possible Root-Cause Event now. Once you have discovered an age, it's time to move on to…

STEP NO. 2 **What Happened?** (Clarify the Context)

Let's find out more information about what happened at the age you've discovered, so that you can establish the Root-Cause Event that was a problem for you. You will do this by clarifying the context: the specific person(s), place, event(s) or thing(s) that were involved. Hold the age you found in Step 1 in your mind while you discover – and trust – your first answers to the following question:

ASK: When I think of that time, what is the first person, place, event or thing to come to mind now? Examples of possible answers include:

- The first **person**: "Dad", "Mum", "Grandfather", "school teacher","brother","best friend".
- The first **place**: "home", "kitchen", "bedroom", "the park near my house", "nursery/school".

- The first **event**: "an argument", "first day of school", "getting lost", "being shouted at", "someone leaving", "getting answer wrong".
- The first **thing**: "my teddy", "Grandmother's perfume", "being cold", "being scared", "box of matches", or any object (an obvious one or a symbolic one) your mind is giving you to help you remember the entire memory.

Remembering the Memory Now

You may by now have recalled a specific detailed memory. If not, then you should focus on remaining open-minded and curious about what might have happened around that time in your life. It can feel as if you are making it up; that's normal. You may need to dig around a bit before the complete memory returns to your conscious awareness. In the same way a detective or an interested friend would ask questions to find out what happened, you might want to also ask:

When I think of this (person, place, etc.), what else comes to mind? Who was there? Where was I? What might have happened in relation to (person, place, etc.) around that time in my life?

For example, if your answer to step 1 was "age four" and your first answer to Step 2 was "Dad", then ask, *When I think about age four and my dad, what else comes to mind?* Or, if your first answer was "box of matches" then ask: *When I think of age four and a box of matches, who or where pops into my mind now? Who else might have been there? What else was going on?*

Like an artist painting a picture, aim to gather as many details as you need to paint an accurate picture of what might have happened. Your goal is to find a memory of an event that could have been a problem for you then. The moment you find a problematic memory immediately go to Step 3 (page 90).

Struggling to Find a Memory? Ask Yourself:

- When in my life did I not have this problem?
- When did I first notice I had this problem?
- How long have I had this problem?
- What was happening during the 12 to 18 month leading up to the first time I noticed the problem?

These questions can give you clues as to the possible Root-Cause Event. For instance, I once asked a client who'd been suffering from migraines, *When did you first notice you had migraines?* She remembered that she'd got her first migraine around the time a friend committed suicide. This then reminded her of an older memory, from when she was 12, when her aunt died suddenly. We worked on healing the age-12 memory, and once we had, she stopped getting migraines.

Still Not Found a Memory? Don't Worry, Try This:

Create an emotional-events events tracker. In a journal, write down, in age order, all the significant emotional events of your life thus far. For example:

> AGE FOUR: Scared leaving Mum at the school gates.
> AGE SEVEN: Sad when best friend moved away.
> AGE EIGHT : Scared when lost at the supermarket.
> AGE TWELVE: Hurt not invited to friend's party.

And so on.

Keep exploring what might have happened until you find a specific event that could have been a problem for you. If you find this impossible, then work on a more recent memory that comes to mind when you think about the physical condition, emotional issue or life problem. Once you have found a problematic memory, you are ready to progress on to...

STEP NO.3 **Why Was It a Problem?** (Find Root-Cause Reason)

Without a time machine, you cannot change what has happened in your past. However, the great news is you don't have to. You can change your *relationship* with what happened. To do this we don't work on *what* happened, but instead, we focus on *why* what happened was a problem for you then. This is a much more effective way to heal past memories because when you heal the reason *why* it was a problem, there is no reason for it be a problem any more.

Find the Root-Cause Reason

The Root-Cause Reason (RCR) is the reason *why* what happened was a problem for you. To discover it you need to explore how you interpreted the past events at the time, the subsequent emotions you felt, and the possible conclusions you came to in light of the emotional events that happened.

Bring to mind the Root-Cause Event you discovered in Steps 1 and 2, so that you can now discover the RCR:

> **FOR EMOTIONS, ASK: What is it about what happened that was a problem for me? How did it make me feel?**
>
> Ask yourself the above questions until you get one or more negative emotions. Then:
>
> **FOR REASONS, ASK: Ultimately, what was it about what happened that caused me to feel that way?**

Keep It Simple

Don't overcomplicate this part of the method. You simply want to consider why you felt the way you did, so you can find the biggest reason for why you felt bad at that moment in your life. Aim to state the Root-Cause Reason in uncomplicated, simple words. Remember that you probably came to the conclusion when you were very young. It can help to include the emotions in the answer to your question by saying:

Ultimately, I felt (sad or scared or angry etc) because… (Say the first reason that comes to mind.)

Once you have the emotion(s) and the reason(s), you are ready to put them together to create the Root-Cause Reason for the problem you want to heal:

Root-Cause Reason Statement

= Emotion(s)	+	Reason(s)
(What you felt)		(Why you felt that way)

(Examples include: "Sad, scared and vulnerable Dad disappeared" or "Angry forced to move house" or "Scared Mum so weak", etc. I have shared approximately 300 real-life Root-Cause Reasons in Appendix 2 to help you fully understand what you are looking for here.)

When you find a Root-Cause Reason, rate it:

> **ASK: On a scale of 0 to 10, with 10 being "very high emotion and feels true", how would I rate (state Root-Cause Reason)?**

Root-Cause Reasons that have the power to justify an unhealthy belief or cause a physical condition or life problem usually have the emotional intensity of 8, 9 or 10 out of 10 (with 10 being high emotion). If your RCR scores 7 or less then you might want to further explore the reasons why what happened was a problem for you, or see if there is a more emotionally significant Root-Cause Event to work on.

∽

Quick Timeout to Check In

By this point in the method you should have discovered a Root-Cause Reason; this is a short sentence that summarizes why the Root-Cause Event was a problem for you then.

Don't forget: just because this sentence may feel true, that does not make it absolutely true. All it means is that the younger you, based on the limited life experience you had at the time, felt justified in feeling bad. If you have found an emotionally charged Root-Cause Reason then great! You are only two steps away from making peace with your past. The hard part of the method is over; now I suggest you go immediately to Chapter 5 to heal it.

Not Found a Root-Cause Reason? Don't Worry!

Turn to Appendix 2 (page 153); you will find I've done all the work for you by revealing the 20 most common unhealthy beliefs and their associated real-life Root-Cause Reasons. Simply read through the list and work on the unhealthy beliefs that feel true to you. Alternatively, another tool for finding your unhealthy beliefs is the "My Incorrect Conclusions" tool on the following page – check it out now.

BONUS TOOL

My Incorrect Conclusions

Remember: all unhealthy beliefs are incorrect conclusions that you've come to at some point in your past. This exercise will help you to discover unhealthy conclusions that you may not even have been aware of believing.

PART NO.1 Starter Sentences

Without editing your thoughts, finish the following sentences with the first words that come to mind. Aim to get a few answers for each starter sentence.

> *I'm...*
> *I'm not...*
> *I always get...*
> *I always feel...*
> *I'm too...*
> *I will never...*
> *It's hard to...*
> *I'm the sort of person who...*

PART NO.2 Life Areas

Now hold the following life areas in your mind and notice the first thoughts you have. For instance, for money, you might have a thought *It's hard to make money* or *I will never get out of debt.* Or, for love/intimacy, you might think *I will never meet my soulmate.* Notice the first thoughts that come to mind when you think about the following areas and note them in a journal:

- Family / friends
- Love / intimacy

- Career / work
- Money / wealth
- Spirituality / enlightenment

NEXT STEPS

Found any unhelpful conclusions after using the first three steps of the Mind Detox Method, the list of top 20 unhealthy beliefs (on page 153) or with the My Incorrect Conclusions tool (on page 93)? Great! Now turn to the next chapter to take positive steps to heal them.

PART THREE

Heal the Hidden Cause

· · · ·

HEAL THE UNHEALTHY BELIEFS THAT ARE CAUSING PHYSICAL, EMOTIONAL AND LIFE PROBLEMS

Heal Your Unhealthy Beliefs

• • • •

THE "RESOLVE" PART OF THE MIND DETOX METHOD

PAY CLOSE ATTENTION! This is a very important moment in your life. Now that you've discovered the Root-Cause Reason(s) that have been justifying one or more unhealthy belief(s), I highly recommend that you immediately move on to heal what you've found.

The purpose of Step 4 of the method is to heal any Root-Cause Reasons that might be justifying the existence of unhealthy beliefs. Remember: problems are only problems today because of the incorrect conclusions you've come to in the past. And the even better news is your unhealthy beliefs are easy to heal because:

REASON NO.1   Beliefs Are Not Absolutely True

Truth is always true. Beliefs are only sometimes correct. Therefore, beliefs can be updated.

REASON NO.2   Beliefs Are Fuelled by Feelings Not Facts

The "realness" of beliefs is based largely on them feeling true, but just because something feels true doesn't make it the truth. Clearing the emotions makes them feel less true for you.

97

REASON NO.3 **Beliefs Are Based Upon Limited Information**

You now know more than you did in the past. With the benefit of hindsight you can think about old events from a more peaceful and compassionate perspective. With new information you can come to new conclusions any time you want.

REMEMBER: It is Never Too Late to Have a Happy Childhood!

You are now going to come to some new, healthier conclusions about the Root-Cause Event and, in the process, let go of any emotions associated with the Root-Cause Reason(s). The goal of this step of the method is to be able to think about the past event and Root-Cause Reason and feel totally neutral.

To be able to feel at peace when thinking about events that used to cause you negative emotions is evidence that any unhealthy belief(s) stemming from the event have been healed. You quite literally no longer believe it is justified to feel bad about what happened. You've evolved beyond it being a problem for you. (Give yourself a pat on the back in advance because you are doing great work!)

Coming to more compassionate conclusions about past events can allow balance to be naturally restored in your body because the reason(s) for the imbalance have been removed.

Your Body Knows How To Heal

Becoming aware of your unhealthy beliefs is the hardest part of the healing process. From now on, your healing journey gets easier. It is the job of your infinitely powerful inner intelligence to take care of the healing details. Your job is to let yourself be at peace with your past – which is easier and less stressful than resisting what happened – so that your mind can give your body the green light for healing to take place.

Remember, the mind–body connection means that changing your mind can cause changes to occur within the body. You may even find that your "inner pharmacy" immediately gets to work healing any physical conditions the moment the new messages start being sent between your mind and body. Sound good? Great, now keep up the brilliant work you've started by moving on to…

STEP NO. 4 **Why Not A Problem Now?** (New Conclusions with New Information)

Hold the Root-Cause Event in your mind as you answer the following question:

What can I know now, that if I had known it in the past I would have never felt (state Root-Cause Reason) in the first place?

You may need to ask yourself this question a few times to explore positive and loving learning. You are looking to find alternative ways of thinking about the old event that would make it impossible to feel bad about what happened. (By this, I'm not saying your goal is to be happy that the bad thing happened, only neutral.) You will know you've found it because you will feel a sense of relief.

Other questions you can ask to explore positive and loving ways of thinking about past events include:

- **What do I need to know or learn, the knowing or learning of which will allow me to be at peace with what happened?**
- **Is it possible for me to be at peace when I think about this event at some point in my life?**
- **Okay, what could I know at that point in the future so that I could feel at peace then?**

- For this to have been a problem then, what did I need to not know? Or, for this to be a problem then, what was I pretending not to know?
- If a friend had this problem, what advice would I give them to help them be more at peace with what happened?
- For me to be at peace with this memory, once and for all, what do I need to say now?

The moment you find a positive and loving learning that makes peace with the original event and disproves the unhealthy belief, move on to Install the Knowing, below.

TOP TOOL Install the Knowing

Timing is everything when installing the knowing. It must be done immediately you discover the learning you need.

It works because any justifications you had in feeling bad about the Root-Cause Event are undermined and stop feeling "true" and you no longer have any justifiable reason to continue feeling bad. You are quite literally taking the newfound positive and loving learning and installing it in your body–mind. It is powerful and, when used correctly, can be very quick and highly effective at completely clearing all negative emotions associated with the Root-Cause Event and Root-Cause Reason, and immediately heal the unhealthy belief.

Steps to Install the Knowing

Get positive and loving learning using Step 4, then:

STEP NO.1 ASK: *Where do I know this in my body?* (Notice where within your own heart, chest, solar plexus and stomach this knowing is in your own body.)

STEP NO. 2 ASK: *If the knowing had a colour, what colour would it be?* (Any colour is fine, so trust your first answer.)

STEP NO. 3 Keep that knowing there and close your eyes. Then use your imagination to go to the past, with that knowing, and play the movie of the old memory from beginning to end, but this time with the new positive and loving learning. For example: I have *the red knowing in my heart that I am loved.* Play the memory from start to finish a couple of times.

STEP NO. 4 Come back to now by opening your eyes. This exercise should take up to 30 seconds.

If the Root-Cause Event is traumatic and you don't want to imagine it happening again, then once you're clear about where in your body the knowing is, progress to using the Emotional Freedom Technique (EFT) to clear the emotions and install the positive learning. See Chapter 7 for full instructions.

Immediately after you have installed the knowing, open your eyes and take your attention away from the problem and memory for a moment by distracting yourself. Look at a picture on the wall, notice something you can hear nearby, or sing a few seconds of a song that lifts your spirits. Do whatever it takes to temporarily take your attention away from what you've been working on. Then, once you've done that, you are ready to move on to the final step of the method…

STEP NO. 5 **Test the Work** (Explore How Emotionally Neutral You Feel)
Testing the work is as important as every other step of the Mind Detox Method. Most people have a convincer of three. By this I mean they need to test the work three different ways for the mind to be

convinced that the change has happened. It is vitally important that your mind feels convinced because this helps to activate the healing process. It also helps the mind to begin proving the new healthier belief right. You will find that, during and after you test the work, your mind will start finding evidence to prove the new belief correct.

Enjoy this natural process and use it to your advantage by consistently acknowledging that the change has happened and that it is now safer and easier for your body to heal. Here's how you test the work:

TEST THE ROOT-CAUSE REASON: On a scale of 10–0, with 0 being "the emotion is completely gone now and I feel neutral", how would I rate the old Root-Cause Reason? (You may want to say the Root-Cause Reason out loud and notice how neutral you feel now.)

TEST THE PAST: On a scale of 10–0, with 0 being "the emotion is completely gone now and I feel neutral", how would I rate the Root-Cause Event? (You might find that the memory is still there, but the old emotion is gone and you now feel more neutral.)

TEST THE FUTURE: Think of a time in the future when "something like this might happen, but this time, notice how differently I respond".

If the answers to the above questions are all 0/10 and you feel neutral, then great. Well done for all the great work you've done and congratulations!

∾

All In One Place

I've put an at-a-glance summary of the 5-Step Method in Appendix 1 (page 149) for quick reference and ease of use. I've also provided a D.I.Y. Mind Detox Tool in Appendix 1 (page 152) for you to use.

Still Feeling Something? Don't Fret!

If you still feel any negative emotions relating to the Root-Cause Event or Root-Cause Reason, it means that there is a part of your mind that still feels justified in feeling bad. This is a blind spot. You need to turn to Chapter 6 to explore my very powerful blind-spot-busting breakthroughs...

CHAPTER SIX

Blind-Spot Busting Breakthroughs

• • • •

HEAL THE HIDDEN REASONS
FOR FEELING BAD

STRUGGLING TO CLEAR NEGATIVE EMOTIONS OR COME TO HEALTHIER CONCLUSIONS? Relax! The following insights are great for healing the more stubborn unhealthy beliefs and emotional events.

Negative emotions exist for a reason. If you have any residual negative feelings about the Root-Cause Event or Root-Cause Reason, it simply means that you have a temporary "blind spot" in your mind. Blind spots are hidden justifications for feeling the way you feel. As long as you have the blind spot, your mind will not let go of all of the negative emotions because it will still believe it is justified in feeling some anger, sadness, fear or other emotion.

Shining a light on the blind spot is as simple as exploring more positive and loving ways of re-remembering the past. When you come to a new conclusion you will naturally feel better because there will be no reason to feel bad any more. It just makes sense.

TOP TIP **Avoid the Common Trap**

My method is entirely focused on healing the mind-based root causes of problems, rather than treating the surface-level symptoms. Negative emotions are caused by your unhealthy beliefs because they are what determines how you feel in relation to what happens in your life. Negative emotions are always only symptoms, never the cause.

Make sure when you're doing this work that you do not fall into the common trap of focusing all of your energy on trying to get rid of the negative emotions. They will go naturally when feeling bad is no longer justified. We only use the emotions as a useful gauge to determine whether or not you've come to new conclusions yet and healed the belief.

(HINT: No Negative Emotion = No Unhealthy Belief)

10 Blind-Spot Busting Breakthroughs

Having worked with literally hundreds of people, I've been privileged to be present when they've been resolving their biggest life problems by having their biggest life breakthroughs. Here are 10 of my favourite blind-spot-busting insights that repeatedly help people to come to more positive and loving conclusions. These blind-spot busters are designed to help you question the assumptions you've been unconsciously making about past events or people. So only keep reading if you're willing to change your opinion about your past and the people in your life!

> *If any of these insights resonate with you to the point that you know it would be impossible to feel bad about the past problem, please immediately use the* **Install the Knowing exercise** *with that insight.*

BLIND SPOT NO.1 **I Survived!**

Fear can be hard to clear if your mind believes *staying scared* is keeping you safe. It isn't! Prolonged fear is harmful to your health. To put your mind at rest, I would like to highlight one very reassuring fact: for you to be reading this book at all means that you survived the significant emotional event(s). Obvious perhaps, but for many people it is a huge *aha* moment they had never considered before.

Consider this: *If you had known, for absolute certain, that you were going to survive the past event, how differently would you have felt at the time?* You might find that you would have been more calm in the knowledge that you were ultimately going to be okay.

Instead of focusing on how scared or vulnerable you may have felt, start to appreciate how resourceful and resilient you *actually* were, and are. After all, you survived! In acknowledging this, you naturally give your mind permission to let go of feelings of hurt, anger, sadness or fear, to be replaced with calmness and the knowledge that everything is going to be okay.

BLIND SPOT NO.2 **I Was Forgetting What Happened Next**

Leading on from Blind-Spot No.1, cast your mind back to a point after the Root-Cause Event when you knew for certain that you were safe and were going to be okay. Although it is natural for the mind to be drawn to think about the most traumatic parts of the past, it is very healing to acknowledge that, although it was traumatic then, you've now ended up safe.

The Dreamer

A good friend of mine had been experiencing intense dreams that would cause him to lash out during sleep. When I asked him the questions from the method, he said he remembered his dad and how angry he was. I then simply asked him *What happened next?* He immediately burst out laughing and said, *Well, nothing!!!* He reported having more deep and peaceful sleep from then on. I believe my friend realizing this allowed his mind to switch off "high-alert mode" and let him enter and enjoy deeper levels of sleep.

But What If Something Bad Did Happen?

I can almost guarantee that there has been a point since the traumatic time when you have become safe again. (Even if that time is right now as you read this page!) Explore focusing more on how safe and well you are *now* rather than how you *were* in the past. Doing so can help your body–mind disengage panic mode and heal more effectively.

BLIND SPOT NO. 3 I Was Doing My Best and So Were They

Inside every human heart is the desire to be happy and to experience love. I've asked literally hundreds of people what they want more than anything else in life. I've asked people with different financial circumstances, religious affiliations, ages and educations. Of these people, how many of them do you think told me they wanted conflict, separation, anger, arguments or anything else negative? That's right, zero. Nobody. *Nada*! Every single person I've asked has wanted positive life experiences, such as peace, happiness, health and love.

> *Everyone wants peace, including the people who do horrible things.*

Blinded by Their Misinformed Mind

I believe that, if given a *genuine* choice (i.e., if they were not being blinded by their own unhealthy beliefs), anyone who has wronged you would always choose options that would move them towards greater happiness, peace and love – if they knew how.

People who don't know how to be at peace, enjoy happiness, or experience love don't need your criticism or anger; they need your compassion. You do not need to agree with their actions, only to understand that, given their own unhealthy beliefs, they were doing their best. Remembering this can help you to see yourself and others from a more gentle, understanding and compassionate perspective.

Are You Being Too Hard on Yourself?

Have you forgotten that you sometimes have to make mistakes in order to learn what is right? Are you ignoring that you were young, innocent, doing your best and, at that point, didn't know any different?

If you are experiencing residual guilt, remember that at the time in your life you did what you did, you would not have done it unless you *believed* it was the best possible option available, given your set of circumstances at that time. There's no point looking back now, from a completely different time and set of circumstances, to judge or feel guilty about what you did in the past. You've since had many life experiences that have shaped you and that would cause you to act differently in similar circumstances today. (Even reading this book makes you a different person to who you were then!) Let learning from it be enough and let go of any guilt.

BLIND SPOT NO. 4 **They Had Their Own Issues to Deal With**

This insight is especially relevant if you felt neglected or let down by your parents when growing up.

As young children we saw our parents as gods. They knew everything, were all-powerful, had no problems and could do absolutely anything. It is only as we grew up to become adults ourselves that we began to appreciate that they were only human and probably had their own difficulties, fears, emotional baggage and stresses to deal with. Furthermore, and at the risk of sounding crude, allow me to highlight an important point. Your parents had sex (or made love, if you prefer), and created a baby. In the moment of conception, they didn't suddenly heal all of their issues or become enlightened; they only became parents. Let's give them a break.

They shouldn't have known better because they couldn't have known better.

By taking into consideration the challenging lives our parents (or other people) had, it can become easier to understand why they left, or why they were moody sometimes, or why they found it hard to love us fully.

Quite remarkably, by acknowledging that other people have their own issues to deal with something magical happens – you stop taking it so personally how they behaved towards you. This enables you to let go of any hurt, sadness, anger, guilt or feelings of being unloved or unwanted and move on, viewing them instead from a more understanding and loving perspective.

BLIND SPOT NO.5 **It Wasn't Personal**

One of the most common reasons for people holding on to negative emotions for years is that they believe the actions of other people have something to do with them. They don't!

Everyone has a unique version of reality. Remember, it works like this: people gather information about their external environment via the five senses. At the point it reaches the mind and nervous system it is raw data, without meaning, just light reflecting off the back of the eye to create pictures and vibration making the eardrum move to produce sound. The unconscious mind then takes that raw data and makes meaning from it by drawing on a unique set of filters, including beliefs, values, past decisions, memories, significant emotional events and so on. This process deletes, distorts and generalizes the data received to create a unique internal version of life.

> *Meaning not only do you see, hear and experience a massively edited version of reality; everyone else on this planet does too!*

Due to everyone having a unique version of reality, most people end up projecting their conditioning out into the world. This causes other people to not necessarily see, hear or experience the REAL you, but only their IDEA of you, based upon *their* internal filters. Get the difference?

Believe it or not, this is great news when it comes to you being able to make peace with your past. It means that you have never (and I mean never) been left, rejected, hated or abandoned by anyone in your past. What your parents or peers or partners have not liked or rejected has only ever been their ideas about you – not you, just their idea, in their mind, based upon their conditioned beliefs, values, memories, significant emotional events and so on. Your mum did not prefer your brother or sister; she only preferred the idea she had in her head about your sibling. Your dad didn't leave you; he left his idea of you, based upon his own issues, conditioning and unhealthy beliefs. Your ex didn't fall out of love with you; he or she came to dislike their idea of you, which was not, and is not, you.

Only an idea! It wasn't personal. What a relief.

∽

A Quick Timeout to Check In

Halfway through the blind-spot busting breakthroughs seems like the perfect moment to take a quick timeout to explore an intriguing observation that can help to undermine the validity of any problem you may be looking to heal.

Here One Minute, Gone the Next

Amongst other adventures, a large part of my life involves travelling the world helping people make peace with the past. Some have been experiencing extreme anger or sadness or fear for decades. Others have resisted life so much and for so long that they have ended up with severe physical conditions. Yet, irrespective of how long difficult event(s) have been a problem for them, there is always a point when they discover a way of thinking about the past that stops it being a problem. In doing so, they end up feeling more neutral or even positive towards life events that, for years, had been causing them intense negative feelings.

Witnessing this in literally hundreds of people led me to begin to question what problems actually are. I mean, if something is a problem for a person for years, and then, after a simple shift in viewpoint, stops being a problem, was it ever a problem in the first place? Or was the real problem the person not yet being able to view the life event(s) from a more positive and conscious perspective?

Stepping Beyond Conditioned Thinking

One of my favourite quotes comes from Albert Einstein and goes: "No problem can be solved with the same level of consciousness that created it". I've observed that it is people's open-mindedness and consciousness that determines whether or not what happens in life is a problem for them. Not the event, but what they think about the event. One person might lose their job and be thrilled at the adventure; another might become physically ill from the stress. The life event is the same, so what's the difference? It's their different perceptions.

Raising your consciousness to ever-increasing heights by bursting through your blind spots is a marvellous thing to do. It can lead you into the direct experience of a life lived free from problems whereby, although unexpected challenges may still arise, you don't experience them as being problems, nor as anything being wrong. How incredible is that? You don't need to wait for anything to change about your past, present or future for you to be able to experience inner peace. When you change your mind, everything changes!

> *Remember, you are not trying to get over problematic life events; rather, you are getting over your conditioned thinking about what's happened.*

Enjoying peace for life becomes easier from this fresh perspective, so let's get back to exploring more blind-spot-busting breakthroughs.

BLIND SPOT NO.6 I've Been Mind-Reading

Have you ever been mean to someone you love? Have you ever even told someone you love that you hate them? Or pushed them away? Or not been there for them when they might have needed you? If you've answered "yes" to any of these questions, then how can you know for certain that if someone shouted at you or was mean to you or wasn't there for you, it automatically meant they didn't love you? That's right, you can't.

One of the most common unhealthy beliefs that cause physical conditions, emotional issues and life problems is the belief *My parents didn't love me enough.* In almost all cases, the belief is based upon a mind-read. By that I mean the person had been reading between the lines, assumed they knew what other people were thinking and concluded the worst.

Then, in a total turnaround in thinking, most people I work with end up realizing that they were in fact loved, very much indeed. In countless cases they recognize that the parent (or whoever) simply didn't know how to express love in a way that made them feel loved. Which, I'm sure you will agree, is something completely different to actually not being loved! For instance, if a child is left by a parent, it is common for the child to come to the conclusion that it means they are not loved or loveable. This simply is not the case. Coming to that conclusion is an assumption based on a mind-read.

> *Irrespective of the actions of another, you can never be
> 100 per cent certain of what is really going on inside
> another person's mind.*

In reality, most people you meet don't even know what's going on in their *own* mind! They are unconsciously acting out their conditioning. So how are *you* supposed to accurately predict *their* thoughts? You're not – so I highly recommend you don't waste your time trying. (And catch yourself when you do.) All you need to know is this: it wasn't personal, and the actions of other people have absolutely no relation to your loveability whatsoever.

Recognizing that a belief or Root-Cause Reason is based upon mind-read assumptions can undermine it, and often causes negative emotions associated with the past to no longer be justified or justifiable.

BLIND SPOT NO. 7 It's Okay For Me to Be Happy

Losing someone you love can often cause feelings of grief. For many, it is a completely natural response. However, if the grief continues too long it can become harmful to the body and limit the vitality and life of the person still living.

People can get stuck in the cycle of grief if they maintain a connection with the person who's died by holding onto the grief, such that if they felt better they would somehow lose or dishonour the person who died. An important question to ask yourself if you're experiencing grief is: *Would my loved one want me to feel sad or experience any other negative emotion because of their death?* You can honour them by loving them while being at peace – as they want you to be.

BLIND SPOT NO. 8 I'm Now Able to Look After Myself

When you were first born you needed your parents completely, to feed you, clean you and protect you. Despite needing your parents when you were very young, you are now at a stage in life when you can feed, clean and look after yourself. An obvious thing to say, perhaps, but for many it is a blind spot. Lots of people continue to hold on to negative emotions towards their parents for not being there for them when they were children. They hold on to the anger, sadness, hurt or fear the child felt – as if they still depend on their parents for their survival.

Now I appreciate that it might have been justifiable to feel these feelings as a child, but as an adult, the emotions are way past their use-by-date!

Waiting For a Past That Never Comes

Subtle ongoing resistance about how your parents were in the past can be destructive to your health, happiness and overall life success today. The resistance is caused by a blind spot in your mind that is still looking to get something from your parents, even if you don't actually need it any more.

Take a moment to fully acknowledge that you are all grown up now. You are able to clothe, feed and look after yourself (even if you don't want to!). You can be safe and survive very well on your own.

Repeat after me…

I can look after myself, I don't need my parents any more and even though I might not necessarily agree with how they raised me, whatever they did worked well at teaching me how to look after myself, be safe and resourceful in this world. Good job, parents!

BLIND SPOT NO.9 Compassion Sets Me Free

Compassion is a combination of unconditional love and wisdom. It is the ability and willingness to love others exactly as they are, in the knowledge that every person on the planet is doing the best they can and wants to experience peace of mind and love.

Being compassionate means that, if someone else is having a hard time or being difficult, you don't join them by feeling bad too. Instead, you stay peaceful within your Real Self (more about this in Part Three) and show them ways to get out of the hole they're in.

Although not feeling bad might sound a bit uncaring at first, it is the only way to truly help others. If you always agree with the other person that they are broken, or get upset with them, you will only reinforce their justifications for being in the hole – which keeps them feeling bad for even longer. I'm sure you don't want that for them, or yourself.

Imagine a friend calls you, upset because they've split up with yet another partner. They tell you, "All men are bastards, let's go out and get drunk!!!" Compassion wouldn't necessarily agree with them, because it might not be useful for them to go on believing that. If this person keeps creating bad relationships, it is more useful to help them see why it's happening and what they can do to enjoy more loving relationships.

Much better to compassionately say what you see, rather than blindly agree with your friend, talk about your failed relationships all night over too much wine and end up with a hangover the next day. (And perhaps even the start of yet another doomed relationship!)

On a more serious note: what if you were abused or attacked? Compassion works in a similar way. Although difficult experiences like these often lead to feelings of hurt, sadness or fear, compassion can set you free from toxic emotions like these.

Rather than getting angry or upset about what someone did, for the sake of your own peace and well-being be willing to view them from a more compassionate perspective. They, like you, want to be happy and know they are loved. Every human, without exception, ultimately wants that; the desire is built in from birth. However, at that time in their lives they didn't know how to love or be happy.

Maybe they had difficult upbringings without any positive role models, so they didn't know how to treat you lovingly? Maybe they didn't love themselves fully and so projected judgements onto you? Or perhaps they were so critical of you because they wanted to make sure you had the opportunities they didn't? Who knows? Don't try to figure it out; doing so would only be a mind-read. Instead, play with seeing the problematic person through more compassionate eyes. You will be amazed at how free you can be.

BLIND SPOT NO.10 To Feel Wanted I Must Want Me First

One of the most common unhealthy beliefs that the Mind Detox Method uncovers is *I'm not wanted*. This belief can come about because a parent has behaved in a way that has made the child feel unwanted, or via a person feeling unwanted by people they have had strong feelings for in intimate relationships. Feeling unwanted often leads to a number of destructive behaviours, causes people to settle for less than they deserve in relationships and overperform to try to earn reassurance from others.

Consider this: *Are you waiting to feel wanted by others when all the time you are not wanting yourself?* You cannot expect anyone else to want you if you don't want you first. Even if other people do want you, if you hold onto the belief that you are not wanted your mind will filter out all the love that you receive from others.

Healing this blind spot requires you to accept the possibility that ultimately nothing is wrong with you. That you can choose to love the skin you're in by appreciating the exquisite beauty of your uniqueness. And most importantly, to let yourself, exactly as you are, be enough. This is a decision that you can make now, without having to wait until you fix, change or improve yourself. Doing so can enable you to find a love within yourself that is beyond the opinions of others.

> *Everything in the cosmos is better off when you give yourself permission to be yourself.*

BONUS BLIND SPOT I Wasn't Being Very Loving Either

Some people hold onto rejection or resentment for years because someone didn't love them in the way they believe they should be loved. They feel fully justified, all this time, in remaining a victim to the other person not loving them enough, not being there for them, not being the parent they'd hoped for and so on. They almost fall off their chair when I ask them: "How good were you at loving your parent (or whoever) unconditionally?"

We then explore: "Is it possible you were waiting to be loved unconditionally, when at the same time you were not loving the other person unconditionally? Did you constantly want the other person to change? Do you want the people in your life to change? Are you imposing your beliefs on the other person? What happens if, right now, you let the other person be enough, exactly as they are? Don't worry, you don't have to love their actions, but for your own sake let yourself love their heart."

What Would Love Do?

Another powerful question you can ask if you ever have a problem with a particular person is *What would Love do now?* Doing so often causes feelings of anger or resentment to fall away and be replaced with gentleness. Love is unconditional, non-judgemental, gives freely and needs absolutely nothing in return.

Remember, you experience love when you give love. Due to this wonderful truth, there is quite literally no limit on the amount of love you can enjoy during your days. Don't wait for someone else to love you before you love them. You might be the very person in their life to show *them* how to love more unconditionally. Be the light that guides others home to the heart.

∾

Getting Your Score to an Absolute Zero

Having installed the relevant blind-spot-busting breakthrough to your Root-Cause Event and Root-Cause Reason, if the scores from questions 5.1 or 5.2 are *above* 0 check the following:

CHECK NO. 1 Antidote Learning

Consider this: *Does the learning I've installed un-justify the negative emotion?* By that I mean: is it the antidote to the reason you felt bad? For instance, if you were "scared of dying", have you installed "I survived"? If you have not installed an antidote learning yet, then consider what learning you need to know now that would completely undermine and un-justify the Root-Cause Reason.

CHECK NO. 2 Root-Cause Reason

Are there more Root-Cause Reasons associated with the Root-Cause Event? Have you worked on the anger you felt, but not addressed the fact that you also felt sad or scared? Consider this: *What else about what happened was a problem for me?* Use the questions in Step No. 3 to explore other Root-Cause Reasons and resolve them using the method.

CHECK NO. 3 Root-Cause Event

Sometimes, multiple events can combine to create an unhealthy belief. In cases like this, there might be another event, perhaps earlier or more recent, that you need to work on now. Consider this: *What other event in my life is the cause of the problem?* Trust your mind to give you other event(s) that need working on so that you can be at peace with the past and heal any unhealthy beliefs that might be negatively impacting your body and life.

∽

MORE TOOLS TO HELP
YOUR HEALING

Whenever faced with more tricky Root-Cause Events and Root-Cause Reasons I will use other healing techniques that I've learned along the way, including:

- Emotional Freedom Technique (EFT)
- Decision Destroyer
- Parts Integration
- Pink Light Technique
- Getting your Goals Process

To discover the power of these additional healing techniques, which can be used alongside the Mind Detox Method, turn to the next two chapters now.

CHAPTER SEVEN

Using Mind Detox with EFT

· · · ·

USING EMOTIONAL FREEDOM TECHNIQUE IN A MORE PRECISE AND POWERFUL WAY

OFTEN DESCRIBED AS PHYSIOLOGICAL ACUPUNCTURE, Emotional Freedom Technique (EFT) is a simple yet highly effective method for clearing blocked emotions. It involves tapping certain points of the body, which correspond with acupuncture points, while saying short statements relating to the problem you wish to release and resolve.

EFT has proven successful in thousands of clinical cases, and I have used it many times to help people to comfortably and quickly let go of all forms of negative emotions, change unhealthy beliefs and even cure health conditions.

Using EFT With My 5-Step Method

One of the most common comments I hear from people using EFT is that they are not sure if they are "tapping on the right problem statement". Or that they feel temporary relief from using EFT, but find that the negative emotions return over time. In my experience, combining EFT with the Mind Detox Method can solve both of these issues.

Tap On the Right Thing

Focusing on getting rid of negative emotions is still working on the symptoms of your problem, not the cause. To totally resolve a problem once and for all, it is vital that you clear the belief-based justifications in your mind. It is your unhealthy beliefs that cause you to resist life and experience negative emotions. As long as your mind believes it is justified in feeling negative when certain circumstances occur, then the problem will appear to "come back" in the future. The reality is that, if you only released emotions but did not heal the unhealthy belief, it was never "fully gone" in the first place.

Instead of tapping on anything and everything, the Mind Detox Method enables you to use EFT in a very precise way. I've found it to be incredibly effective to tap on the Root-Cause Reason statements you discover using my method. This can help to release the justifications in your mind for feeling bad, and is very effective in making peace with your past and enjoying long-term freedom from problems.

INSTRUCTIONS

Once you've clarified the Root-Cause Reason (using Steps 1–3 of my method), follow these steps:

STEP NO.1 **The Set-Up Statement**

While tapping the Karate Chop (KC) point located on the side of the hand (see Diagram 1), repeat the set-up statement three times:

> *Even though I (*state Root-Cause Reason*), I love and accept myself.* For example: *Even though I'm sad my dad left, I love and accept myself.*

STEP NO. 2 **The Round of Tapping**

Tap seven to nine times on each of the meridian points while repeating the Root-Cause Reason at each point (see Diagram 1 on page 127 for location of meridian points).

AT-A-GLANCE LIST OF MERIDIAN POINTS

1 - TH: top of head	8 - AP: armpit
2 - EB: eyebrow	9 - L: liver
3 - SE: side of eye	10 - TH: thumb
4 - UE: under eye	11 - IF: index finger
5 - UN: under nose	12 - MF: middle finger
6 - CH: chin	13 - LF: little finger
7 - CB: collarbone	14 - KC: karate

STEP NO. 3 **Repeat Round with Positive Learning**

Tap seven to nine times on each of the meridian points (TH to LF) again, but this time feel free to say positive learning (see Chapter 6 for suggestions) on some of the points – this can help you to "tap in" healthier conclusions.

STEP NO. 4 **Re-Rate Emotional Intensity**

Take a deep breath and measure the problem again, using the Step 5 questions from my method:

TEST THE ROOT-CAUSE REASON

On a scale of 10–0, with 0 being "The emotion is completely gone now and I feel neutral", how would I rate the old Root-Cause Reason?

TEST THE PAST: On a scale of 10–0, with 0 being "the emotion is completely gone now and I feel neutral", how would I rate the Root-Cause Event?

TEST THE FUTURE: I think of a time in the future when something like this could happen, but this time, notice how differently I respond.

If your score is higher than 0, repeat the sequence from 1–5 with the new set-up statement:

Even though I still feel "sad Dad left" I deeply and completely love and accept, appreciate and respect, honour and forgive myself. Then on each point, say *Remaining "sadness about Dad leaving"*, for example.

Remember: if after doing EFT the emotion stays above 0 it means you have a blind spot justifying the emotion; in this case explore Chapter 6 and install the learning you need so you no longer feel justified in feeling any negative emotions associated with the RCE or RCR. Alternatively, turn to Chapter 8, where you will find additional techniques for healing.

Diagram 1: EFT Points

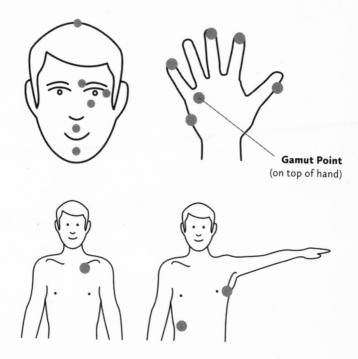

Gamut Point
(on top of hand)

CHAPTER EIGHT

Top Tools to Help Healing

• • • •

MORE RESOURCES FOR ENHANCED RESULTS

THIS CHAPTER INCLUDES ADDITIONAL TOOLS AND TECHNIQUES that I use with great success at my Mind Detox clinics and retreats, including:

- Decision Destroyer
- Parts Integration
- Pink Light Technique
- Getting Your Goals Process

As a quick summary, the Decision Destroyer helps to heal unhealthy beliefs. The Parts Integration helps you to find and integrate any conflicting parts in your mind that could stop you from getting your score to a zero. The Pink Light Technique heals your relationship with yourself and others through the most powerful healing force on the planet – love. And finally, the Getting Your Goals Process clears the mind-based blockages that might prevent you from enjoying the life success you want.

TOOL NO.1 **Decision Destroyer**

Imagine you catch yourself (or a friend) saying an unhealthy belief like, "People I love leave" or "It's hard to make money" or "I can't lose weight". There are a couple of questions you can ask to challenge the unhealthy belief and, in some cases, completely heal it in seconds.

The interesting thing about beliefs is that there was often a moment prior to forming the belief when you either consciously or unconsciously made a decision. This means that many unhealthy beliefs are preceded by, or based on, an unhealthy decision. This exercise can help you to go back in time (in your mind), make a more positive decision and, as a result, form a more healthy belief.

INSTRUCTIONS

Temporarily hold the unhelpful belief in your mind whilst trusting your first answer to the question: *When did I decide that?*

You may get a number and/or a memory pop into your mind. Amazingly, most people I ask this question of immediately remember the exact moment they formed the unhealthy belief. Once you have a possible memory, ask: *What was I deciding before that?*

Keep asking the second question (going earlier and earlier in time) until you find a decision that is purely positive and loving. It may feel as though you are making it up and that there is no way of genuinely knowing what you were thinking then; this is completely normal. The purpose of this exercise is to track back in your mind until you come across a more positive decision. (Which is probably going to be the opposite of the unhelpful belief!) Then take a deep breath and come back to now, bringing the positive decision with you. Trust your unconscious mind to do this for you. You may now find that, if you think about the old unhealthy belief, it feels less true.

TOP TIP **Family Friendly**

This is a great tool that can be used very casually with your kids over the kitchen table or with a friend over a cup of tea. Give it a go and have fun!

TOOL NO. 2 **Parts Integration**

One of the most common blocks to healing the Root-Cause Event or Root-Cause Reason is what's called a Parts Conflict. You have a parts conflict if a part of you wants to let go of the problem and a part wants to hold on. The part that wants to hold on is like a weed: It can grow with time and the problem can return. If you think a parts conflict might be blocking your healing, use this Parts Integration tool.

INSTRUCTIONS

STEP NO. 1 **Invite the Negative Part Out**

Say: "I would like to invite out on to the palm of one of my hands the part that wants to hold on to the problem." Then hold one of your hands out in front of you, palm facing upwards, as though the part has come out and is sitting on the palm of your hand.

STEP NO. 2 **Invite the Positive Part Out**

Now invite out the part that wants to let go of the problem. Say: "I would like to invite out onto the palm of my other hand the part that wants to let go of the problem." By this point you should have both of your hands out in front of you, with one part sitting on one hand and the other part on the other hand.

STEP NO. 3 **Find the Highest Intention of the Negative Part**

Each of the parts has a positive highest intention. Starting with the negative part, ask: "For what purpose does this part exist?" Keep asking: "For what purpose… (including your previous answer in the question)" until you find a positive intention for the negative part. For example: "For what purpose hold on to the fear of failure?" Keep asking and you might find that the intention is to "stay safe", so that you "survive", can "keep living", have a "good life" or so you ultimately "feel happy". By this rationale, the highest intention is to be happy.

STEP NO. 4 Find the Highest Intention of the Positive Part

Do the same with the positive part until you find the *same* highest intention. Ask: "For what purpose does this part exist?" Keep asking: "For what purpose…? (including your previous answer in the question)" until you find a positive intention for the negative part. For example: "For what purpose let go of the fear of failure?" Keep asking and you might find that the intention is to "go for what you want", so you are "more adventurous", "explore more" and finally so you ultimately "feel happy". By this rationale, the highest intention is to be happy.

STEP NO. 5 Put the Highest Positive Intention Inside

Place the integrated highest intention back into the body (in whatever location feels right) and install it with deep breath.

STEP NO. 6 Re-Test the Work

Retest the work using Step 5 from the Mind Detox Method. You may find that the emotions now feel neutral or even positive.

TOOL NO. 3 Pink Light Technique

This technique is ancient in origin and can be used to heal relationships. It is used to heal all pain and suffering between the user and the subject. It has never been known to fail.

INSTRUCTIONS

STEP NO.1 Get yourself in a loving space. Remember a time when you felt loved.

STEP NO.2 In your mind's eye, picture pink loving light radiating from your heart, encompassing you in a pink sphere.

STEP NO.3 Stay within your pink light sphere. Remember a most loving memory of yourself (this could be recent or from your childhood) and project this aspect of you outside the pink light sphere. Cover this projection of yourself with the pink loving light, still radiating from your heart.

STEP NO.4 Then, starting with your immediate family—mother, father, siblings, partner, children—imagine them appearing individually in front of you, outside the pink light sphere. If possible, make it an image of them in a loving memory. In your mind's eye, picture yourself covering each of them with the pink light as if you were icing a cake. Cover them with light and then let them go and move on to the next person. If there is someone who you cannot remember as part of a loving memory, just picture them in front of you. If you cannot do this, visualize bringing them in to stand at a distance and/or facing away from you.

STEP NO.5 Next, do this with anyone with whom you still have an emotional charge or discomfort.

STEP NO.6 Allow for anyone else to show up (whether you know them or not), cover them with the pink loving light and let them go as well.

NOTE: In the beginning, this process should take no more than 10 minutes a day, eventually getting down to five minutes. If you can't visualize the pink light, that's fine; what is important is the intent. Once someone is done, assume that they are finished for the day. You will get a sense of when someone is "complete" and no longer requires a treatment. Some people will not show up for a while; others, who you didn't expect to see, will suddenly appear to receive their pink light.

This technique has been highly successful for people who have been raped, molested or abused. Runaway children have been known to reconnect with their family within weeks of starting to use it. Although most people using this technique find it easy to do, some – principally, in my experience, cancer patients – can have difficulty doing Step 3. Be gentle on yourself and enjoy the results.

TOOL NO.4 Achieving Your Goals Process

Beliefs can either help or hinder you. This tool helps you to, first, rate your current level of belief in your ability to achieve your goal. Then, if you discover you don't fully believe it is possible for you, you should use the Mind Detox Method to heal the unhelpful belief before going on to do a lovely visualization to help install it in your future.

INSTRUCTIONS

STEP NO.1 Clarify Your Goal

Clarity is power. What do you want? Do you want to meet a life partner, make more money, enhance your health, improve a relationship or something else? State your desired outcome now.

STEP NO.2 Rate Your Current Belief Level

On a scale of 0–10, with 10 being that you believe it is possible to achieve your goal, how would you rate your current level of belief?

If you do not rate it as 10 out of 10, you might have an unhelpful belief that is undermining your ability to achieve your goal. Continue on to Steps 3–5 to detox your unhelpful belief. Or, if you score 10 out of 10 and achieving your goal already feels inevitable, go straight to step 6.

STEP NO. 3 **Clarify Your Unhelpful Belief(s)**
What are the first thoughts that come to mind when you think about achieving your goal? Examples of unhelpful beliefs include: *I'm not loveable*, *It's hard to make money* and *I will never heal*. You are aiming to find possible beliefs that could be preventing you from achieving your goal.

STEP NO. 4 **Heal Your Belief(s)**

4.1 What event in your life is the cause of your unhelpful belief, the first event that, when resolved, will cause the belief to disappear? What age were you? Trust your first answer. State your age now.

4.2 When you think of that time, what is the first person, place, event or thing to come to mind? Trust your first answer and let the memory come back to you now.

4.3.1 What is it about what happened that was a problem for you? How did what happened make you feel?

4.3.2 Ultimately, what was it about what happened that was a problem for you? Write down the Root-Cause Reason now in one sentence: – emotion + reason.

4.3.3 On a scale of 0–10, with 10 being "high emotion and feels true", how would you rate your Root-Cause Reason?

4.4.1 What do you know now that, if you had known it in the past, you would never have (state Root-Cause Reason) in the first place?

4.4.2   For this to have not been a problem then, what would you have needed to believe?

Use Install the Knowing Exercise now, using the instructions on page 100.

4.5.1   Test RCR: On a scale of 10–0, with 0 being "the emotion is completely gone now and I feel neutral", how do I rate the old Root-Cause Reason?

4.5.2   Test the past: On a scale of 10–0, with 0 being "the emotion is completely gone now and I feel neutral", how would I rate the Root-Cause Event?

4.5.3   Test the future: Think of a time in the future when something like this could happen, but this time, notice how differently I respond.

STEP NO. 5 **Install a Goal in Your Future**

This final step takes about one minute and is to be done 2–3 times every day until the goal is accomplished. By doing so you will send a consistent message to your body-world about what it is you want.

5.1   Imagine what you will see, hear, feel, smell and taste when you have achieved your goal.

5.2   Cup your hands in front of you and imagine gently placing the image of what you want in the palm of your hand.

5.3   For a few moments, appreciate it now, as if you've already attracted it into your life.

5.4   Breathe three deep breaths of life into the image of what you want.

5.5   Now, imagine the image of what you want effortlessly rising and flying into your future to manifest at a time that is most perfect for you.

*"Until one is committed, there is hesitancy,
the chance to draw back—Concerning all acts of
initiative (and creation), there is one elementary
truth that ignorance of which kills countless ideas
and splendid plans: that the moment one definitely
commits oneself, then Providence moves too.
All sorts of things occur to help one that would
never otherwise have occurred. A whole stream of
events issues from the decision, raising in one's favor
all manner of unforeseen incidents and meetings
and material assistance, which no man could have
dreamed would have come his way. Whatever you
can do, or dream you can do, begin it. Boldness has
genius, power, and magic in it. Begin it now."*

GOETHE

The Ultimate
Mind Detox

. . . .

LOVE HEALS EVERYTHING

The Ultimate Mind Detox

. . . .

KNOW YOU ARE ONE WITH LOVE

WANTING TO BE LOVED AND FEELING LET DOWN in some way sits at the heart of the problems of most of the people I've worked with using the Mind Detox Method. Irrespective of what the presenting problem is, whether that be a physical condition, emotional issue or life challenge, the antidote is very often love. Irrespective of how traumatic the past significant emotional event happens to have been, again the antidote is love. And irrespective of the country, culture, age or background of the people from around the globe I've worked with, love appears to be by far the most powerful force on the planet for bringing about miraculous healings. It, therefore, seems apt to close this book with an exploration into bringing more love into your life.

Looking for Love in the Wrong Places

Most people I meet were, when growing up, encouraged to look for love on the outside. In a very innocent way (because they didn't know any better), parents, teachers and peers tend to act in ways that give the impression that love is something you "get" from the outside, rather than a gentle presence that resides within you, always.

Due to this conditioning, it is common to fall into the trap of working hard to "get" love by having the right kind of body, building a successful career, being surrounded by friends and family and, of course, by finding that special someone. Although all of these things can be lovely, looking to them as your *source of love* can lead to frustration, fear, hurt, sadness and loneliness, and cause a huge amount of unnecessary stress and suffering. Not only that, but due to the unhealthy belief that love is attained by acting a certain way, many people can unintentionally start "performing" to be loveable. They mould themselves to meet the expectations of others and society, and in the process lose their uniqueness by trying to fit in.

The Ultimate Life Lesson

Based on the hundreds of Mind Detox consultations that I've conducted at my clinics and retreats, I've observed one core belief that sits at the heart of most people's problems: the belief that they are separate from the inner source of love, and therefore have to *do* something to *be* loveable or "get" love. This belief, which is usually formed early on in life, makes people look for love on the outside. They believe that they have to prove their loveability by looking and acting a certain way. And even if they do get love from external sources, they often end up being disappointed—not because they aren't loved, but because the "outside love" is never as intimate or as fulfilling as the love found within their own hearts. As a natural consequence, making it a priority to find love within appears to be the ultimate life lesson that most people I meet need to learn at some point in their life.

Take Your Healing Journey to New Heights

Discovering that you are not separate from love can reap rapid rewards. Rather than having to change yourself so that you can *even-*

tually feel loved, you can *immediately* connect with an inner presence of love right now. Take a moment to consider the implications of this remarkable possibility. You don't need to fix, change and improve yourself (or others), so that one day you can experience love. Instead, love comes built in, and enjoying your birthright can be as immediate as tapping into an inner love that is *already* present.

> *Stop trying to be loved and, instead,*
> *discover that you are love.*

Imagine if you knew that love was forever within you and that you went about your days experiencing the presence of love within. How differently would you live your life? Would you be so concerned about being seen as successful? Would you worry about what people thought of you? Would you stay in a job that didn't make you happy? Would you spend time with people who didn't treat you well? Or would you feel freer to be, do and have what makes your heart sing?

Stop Needing Reasons to Love

The love you want is unconditional. It isn't based on you looking a certain way, living up to a specific standard or performing in any particular manner. Love is your birthright as a human being.

> *Love comes from allowing "what is" right now.*

One of the quickest ways to immediately enjoy more love is to play with letting go of needing reasons to love – by letting yourself and your life be good enough, exactly as it is. You feel love when you give love; meaning that the more love you are willing to give, the more love you get to enjoy. By letting go of conditions, you naturally allow for more opportunities to love. Explore this delightful possibility with the following games:

GAME NO.1 **Perfectly Imperfect**

This game can help you to take a break from judging yourself as good or bad, right or wrong, loveable or unloveable. The good news is that there is no tablet of stone somewhere that states how you *should* be. So however you or your life is right now is perfectly imperfect.

> *Your idea that life needs to be different before it's fully*
> *loveable is exactly that – an idea.*
> *Let it go to let love flow.*

CONSIDER THIS: Do you have an idea of your ideal life? Is there a gap between how things are now and how you think things should be? If life doesn't match up to your mind-based ideal scenarios then you can end up unnecessarily postponing loving it.

On a piece of paper, draw a line down the middle of the page. On one side of the page write down how you, your body and your life circumstances are today. Then, on the other side of the paper write down how you think you, your body and your life circumstances *should* be. Then, know this: although you may have an idea of your super self and your ideal life, you are not failing or any less loveable if you don't match up to your mind-based conditions.

Take a moment now to let your body, career, finances, relationships and life be enough exactly as they all are. If they were meant to be any other way then they would be. They might change in the future, but reconnecting with love now involves you letting this moment be enough. Take a break from things needing to be fixed, changed, different, or improved. Just allow what you are and let whatever is happening be as it is now. As you do this, you might notice a sense of relief and relaxation within your being; as you explore it more, you may well find that the essence of your being is love.

GAME NO.2 One Love

Although it may feel as though you experience positive and negative emotions, it can be very liberating to be open to the possibility that there is ultimately only one energy within you. The only change is that it fluctuates in intensity. Yes, I appreciate that there are times when the inner loving energy is subtle and times when it is intense. And, of course, times when it feels good and times when it feels uncomfortable.

Nevertheless, consider this: Would you resist what you are currently feeling if you knew it was love? What if you are being loved from within? Would you resist the loving energy or would you allow it to exist within you?

Place your hand on your heart, breathe deeply and allow yourself to experience whatever emotions you are feeling as you would if you already knew that this energy is the presence of love within.

GAME NO.3 Om Love Meditation

Personally I have discovered the inner source of love through my daily practice of meditation. Meditating regularly allows you to become more aware of the presence of your inner being. You can discover that the essence of your being is love.

There's No Place Like Om

Om is the vibration of creation. Om is known as being the very first movement from stillness, the first sound that comes from silence, and the first something that comes from the nothing. Thoughts, on the other hand, are in essence unmanifested potentiality. They are the seeds of creation. As a result, your thoughts are one of the most powerful tools you have to bring what you want into creation.

To align your attention with Om is to align your attention with the infinite power of creation. It can be incredibly powerful. Whatever thoughts you marry Om up with in your mind can help bring them into creation. To harness the power of Om you can use what I call an "Om Thought". If you want more love, "Om Love" is a very powerful Om Thought to use.

For the best results, think "Om Love", with your eyes open, throughout your day. Do not repeat it non-stop as you would a mantra, just think it occasionally whenever you remember to do so. You are not trying to force a feeling; it works even if you think or feel that it isn't. Every time you think it you are watering the seeds of your intentions by aligning your attention with the power of the universe. Below are instructions for closed-eyes meditation.

CLOSED-EYES MEDITATION

STEP NO.1 Be Comfortable

Sit comfortably on a seat, sofa or even on your bed. Wear loose clothes, support yourself with cushions and wrap yourself in a blanket if there's a chance you could get chilly. Quite simply, be comfortable.

STEP NO.2 Be Allowing

Gently close your eyes while remaining alert. From the here and now, let your attention rest wide as you watch whatever is happening within your mind, right now. This takes no effort, no straining or trying. Continue by very easily, comfortably and gently observing your thoughts as they flow through your mind – as though they were passing clouds in the vast sky.

STEP NO.3 Be Loving

Gently think "Om Love", then let the thought go. Do not try to hold it in your mind. Just stay alert and watch whatever is happening within your awareness. After a while you will notice that your mind has become active and that you have started thinking. This is natural and a deeply ingrained habit, so go easy on yourself. When you notice that you've been thinking, gently rethink "Om Love". For the rest of your time meditating, slowly go between being aware, thinking "Om Love", being aware as you wait until you start thinking, then rethinking your "Om Love", being aware… and so on. Go back and forth, in a very easy and comfortable way. This enjoyable meditation technique can you help you to rediscover the love that lives within you.

Living in Love

Everything exists within a constant context of love. By bringing your attention back to the present moment you can discover an inner presence. The more you practise with the games provided, the clearer it becomes that the presence you are experiencing is love: unbounded, undiluted, unconditional love. When you are resting, fully aware of your being, you live in love and events that you used to see as problems become opportunities for you to learn how to love more unconditionally.

Knowing you are one
with the inner source of love
is by far the most effective way to
heal the hidden cause.

The 5-Step Method
• • • •
AT A GLANCE

Key to Important Terms

ROOT-CAUSE EVENT
The significant emotional event in your past.

ROOT-CAUSE CONCLUSION
The conclusion you came to as a result of the Root-Cause Event happening.

ROOT-CAUSE REASON
The reason why the Root-Cause Event was a problem for you. It is a short sentence with an emotional element and the main reason(s) why you felt the way you did.

UNHEALTHY BELIEF
This is the same as the Root-Cause Conclusion. I use the word "beliefs" because readers are more familiar with the term. You will discover that all unhealthy beliefs stem from one or more corresponding Root-Cause Reason(s).

THE 5-STEP METHOD AT A GLANCE

PART ONE **DISCOVER the Unhealthy Beliefs**

1.   **Find Root-Cause Event** *(WHEN did it start?)*
     ASK: What event in my life is the cause of the problem,
     the first event which, when resolved, will cause the problem
     to disappear? If I were to know, what age was I?

2.   **Clarify the Context** *(WHAT happened?)*
     ASK: When I think of that time, what's the first person,
     place, event or thing to come to mind?
     Digging-deeper questions: Who was there? Where was
     I? What was happening?

3.   **Discover the Root-Cause Reason** *(WHY was it a
     problem?)*

3.1 FOR EMOTION – ASK: What is it about what hap-
     pened that was a problem for me? How did it make me
     feel?

3.2 FOR REASON – ASK: Ultimately, what was it about
     what happened that caused me to feel that way?

3.3 RATE ROOT-CAUSE REASON – ASK: On a scale
     of 0–10, with 10 being "very high and feels true", how
     would I rate (state Root-Cause Reason)?

PART TWO **HEAL the Unhealthy Beliefs**

4.   **Come to New Conclusions with New Info**
     (WHY IS IT NOT a problem now?)

4.1 LEARN FROM THE PAST – ASK: What can I know
     now, that if I had known it in the past, I would have never
     felt (state Root-Cause Reason) in the first place?

4.2 LEARN FROM THE FUTURE – ASK: Is it possible
     that I can be at peace when I think about this old event
     at some point in my life? If yes, when? Okay, what will

I know at that point in the future that will enable me to feel at peace then?

4.3 LEARN FROM THE BLIND SPOT – ASK: For this to have been a problem, what did I need to not know? Digging-deeper question: For it to be a problem then, what did I need to believe? (Helps finds conclusion)

Use the Install the Knowing exercise when you discover a positive and loving learning that makes it impossible for you to have negative emotions associated with the RCE or RCR.

PART THREE **TEST the Work**

5. **Test that the RCR is Resolved**
   (Acknowledge Emotional Domino Benefits)

5.1 TEST THE RCR: On a scale of 10–0, with 0 being "the emotion is completely gone now and I feel neutral", how do I rate the old Root-Cause Reason?

5.2 TEST THE PAST: On a scale of 10–0, with 0 being "the emotion is completely gone now and I feel neutral", how would I rate the Root-Cause Event?

5.3 TEST THE FUTURE: Think of a time in the future when something like this could happen, but this time, notice how differently I respond?

D.I.Y. MIND DETOX

WHEN **Find Age**	What event in my life is the cause of the problem, the first event that when resolved, will cause my problem to disappear? If I were to know, what age was I?
WHAT **Root Cause**	When I think of that time, what's the first person, place, event or thing that comes to mind?
WHY **Root-Cause Reason**	How did what happened make me feel? Ultimately, what was it about what happened that caused me to feel that way?
WHY NOT **Loving Learning**	What can I know now, that if I had known it in the past, I would have never felt any negative emotions in the first place?
Now use the Install the Knowing exercise	

The Top 20 Unhealthy Beliefs

• • • •

(WITH ASSOCIATED ROOT-CAUSE REASONS)

Irrespective of what the physical, emotional or life problem is, during literally hundreds of Mind Detox consultations I've observed the same unhealthy beliefs appearing time and time again.

The top 20 most common unhealthy beliefs are shared over the following pages. Making sure you don't believe any of them can help you to heal current problems and prevent the onset of future ones.

THE CLAIM

How can I make the claim that these unhealthy beliefs have the potential to cause physical conditions? Here's how:

1. When I met clients at my clinics, workshops or residential retreats they had a physical condition;

2. After the consultation(s) many clients reported their physical conditions getting better;

3. The only thing we did during the consultation(s) was to help them make peace with their past by discovering and healing their hidden unhealthy beliefs and associated Root-Cause Reasons.

How to Use the List

Unhealthy beliefs have Root-Cause Reasons (RCR) that provide mental and emotional evidence that justifies them being true (for you). If you find an unhealthy belief in the Top 20 list that feels true, you then want to find the corresponding RCR(s) that are justifying the belief.

Follow these Steps:

1. Read the list of unhealthy beliefs and notice whether any of them feel true to you and/or if you have evidence that proves their validity.

2. Once you discover an unhealthy belief that resonates with you, turn to the subsequent pages to find real-life examples of Root-Cause Reasons (RCR) that, in my experience, I've found to be justifying the unhealthy belief.

3. Read through the list to find the RCR that most resonates with you. Place a tick in the box beside it. You may notice while reading through that an RCR of your own comes to mind that better fits your personal experience. Write it down if it does.

4. Once you've discovered the unhealthy belief and corresponding RCR, do your best to remember a problematic event from the past that is linked with the RCR. For instance, if your RCR is "sad I'm bad", then think of a memory in the past when you felt sad because you thought you'd been bad. Having a memory is useful when it comes to healing the belief.

5. Once you have the unhealthy belief, RCR and memory, go to Chapter 5 to learn how to can achieve peace with your past.

Reality Is What Is Real Right Now

All you are exploring and changing here is your imagination. You are not time-travelling, and your past is no longer happening. Right now you are safe, and you will remain so throughout. These unhealthy beliefs may feel true, but they are not absolutely true.

Remembering this can help the entire process be comfortable – and even enjoyable! If you are in any doubt about your ability to go through this process on your own, please consult a qualified Mind Detox practitioner (by using the Practitioner Finder at *www.minddetox.com*).

TOP 20 UNHEALTHY BELIEFS

1. "My parents didn't love me enough".
2. "I'm unloved".
3. "I'm unwanted".
4. "I'm rejected".
5. "I'm on my own".
6. "I'm abandoned".
7. "Someone important left me".
8. "There's nobody there for me".
9. "I'm alone, lonely and/or isolated".
10. "There is something wrong with me".
11. "I'm bad".
12. "I'm not good enough".
13. "I've let others down".
14. "I'm let down by others".
15. "It should not have happened that way".
16. "I've lost someone/something I love".
17. "I feel bad for others".
18. "I'm not able to do what I want".
19. "I'm unprotected, unsafe and/or vulnerable".
20. "I can't stop bad things happening".

Other Common Unhealthy Beliefs Include:

"There's something wrong".

"I'm weak".

"I'm confused".

"It's my fault".

"I'm separate from the source of love".

Real-life Root-Cause Reasons justifying the most common un-healthy beliefs:

Important: It is *not* recommended that you read through all of the following Root-Cause Reasons: they do not necessarily make for light reading! Just read the examples listed below the unhealthy belief(s) that feel most true to you.

1. Real-life Root-Cause Reasons justifying the belief
    My parents did not love me enough include:

☐ "Sad not loved by Mum and Dad".
☐ "Hurt that Dad loves Mum more than me".
☐ "Sad Mum and Dad didn't care enough".
☐ "Sad, scared and vulnerable my parents didn't care about me".
☐ "Sad and vulnerable Dad didn't love me".
☐ "Hurt, sad and rejected Mum and Dad loved my brother more".
☐ "Sad, hurt and abandoned not cared about".
☐ "Sad Dad doesn't love me".
☐ "Sad Mum and Dad couldn't be bothered helping me".
☐ "Hurt, sad and scared Mum didn't want me".
☐ "Sad, scared and vulnerable Dad didn't fight for me".
☐ "Sad, alone and left out parents didn't love me as much".
☐ "Hurt, sad and vulnerable Mum didn't love me".
☐ "Sad my parents preferred my brother".
☐ "Sad I don't feel loved and supported by Mum and Dad".
☐ "Hurt that my mum and dad resent me".
☐ "Angry and sad Mum and Dad didn't give a shit about me".
☐ "Sad Dad doesn't love me for who I am".
☐ "Hurt Mum didn't tell me she loved me".

2.　　Real-life Root-Cause Reasons justifying the belief
　　　I'm unloved include:

☐　"Left out and lonely not loved as much".
☐　"Hurt and angry not cared about".
☐　"Sad and alone not loved".
☐　"Sad I don't matter".
☐　"Alone and lonely because I'm not loveable".
☐　"Scared of not being loved".
☐　"Sad I don't know why I'm not liked".
☐　"Sad and scared not liked".
☐　"Sad, scared and vulnerable not loved by Mum".
☐　"I need to work hard in order to be loved".
☐　"Sad and useless not loveable as I am".
☐　"Hurt, sad and scared not loveable".

3.　　Real-life Root-Cause Reasons justifying the belief
　　　I'm unwanted include:

☐　"Sad treated so unfairly all the time because I'm not wanted".
☐　"Hurt and worthless not loved and accepted for who I am".
☐　"Hurt Mum and Dad didn't accept me".
☐　"Sad that I'm not wanted".
☐　"Scared that I'm not needed".
☐　"Empty because I don't matter".
☐　"Sad, vulnerable and scared that nobody wants me".
☐　"Lonely and isolated never good enough to have a best friend".
☐　"Hurt that I'm not noticed".
☐　"Feel worthless and not wanted".
☐　"Sad and angry that I don't matter".

- [ ] "Sad and worthless when people are happy without me".
- [ ] "Scared and alone because I'm not wanted".
- [ ] "Sad unwanted because I was a girl".
- [ ] "Hurt there's something wrong with me and I'm not wanted".
- [ ] "Sad Dad didn't want me".
- [ ] "Sad parents didn't want me".
- [ ] "Hurt, sad and vulnerable Mum and Dad sent me away".

4.   Real-life Root-Cause Reasons justifying the belief *I'm rejected* include:

- [ ] "Hurt and rejected by people".
- [ ] "Hurt, rejected and worthless Mum doesn't love me".
- [ ] "Scared of being hurt and rejected by someone I love".
- [ ] "Sad, angry and worthless I was rejected and replaced".
- [ ] "Hurt and rejected because I was a girl".
- [ ] "Sad and rejected when misunderstood".
- [ ] "Sad my brother rejected me".
- [ ] "Sad rejected by Mum".
- [ ] "Sad, hurt, unwanted and rejected when people leave me".
- [ ] "Hurt rejected by my dad".

5.   Real-life Root-Cause Reasons justifying the belief *I'm on my own* include:

- [ ] "Left out and alone".
- [ ] "Sad, scared & vulnerable on my own".
- [ ] "Scared when I'm on my own".
- [ ] "Lost, alone and lonely on my own".
- [ ] "Sad they are going to leave me on my own".

- ☐ "Scared and alone left on my own".
- ☐ "Isolated and vulnerable I'm on my own".
- ☐ "Helpless completely on my own".
- ☐ "Sad about being left out".
- ☐ "Sad, sick and lonely when I'm left to survive on my own".
- ☐ "Let down, lost and lonely left to get by on my own".
- ☐ "Sad, lonely, left alone and having to do things on my own".

6. Real-life Root-Cause Reasons justifying the belief
    I'm abandoned include:

- ☐ "Scared of being abandoned".
- ☐ "Sad everyone I love abandons me".
- ☐ "Sad and scared abandoned by my mum".
- ☐ "Hurt and angry that I was abandoned".
- ☐ "Abandoned in my moment of need".
- ☐ "Completely lost and abandoned not cared about".
- ☐ "Sad, lonely and helpless when abandoned and left behind".
- ☐ "Alone and abandoned not cared about".
- ☐ "Sad, shocked and confused abandoned by Mum".
- ☐ "Hurt, sad and scared not safe abandoned by Mum".
- ☐ "Terrified abandoned by Mum".

7. Real-life Root-Cause Reasons justifying the belief
    Someone important left me include:

- ☐ "Hurt, scared and alone when Mum left".
- ☐ "Sad Dad left me behind".
- ☐ "Sad, scared, alone and vulnerable when Dad left me".
- ☐ "Hurt and angry Mum and Dad left us".
- ☐ "Scared and hopeless when people I love leave".

☐ "Sad I miss the people I love".
☐ "Sad, scared and vulnerable parents left me on my own".
☐ "Sad, hurt and unwanted when people leave me".

8.   Real-life Root-Cause Reasons justifying the belief
     There's nobody there for me include:

☐ "Sad nobody there for me".
☐ "Sad Dad wasn't there for me".
☐ "Sad, weak and rejected nobody there for me".
☐ "Sad and alone without my soulmate there for me".
☐ "Lost and alone nobody there for me".
☐ "Sad and lonely nobody there for me".
☐ "Sad, scared and vulnerable not looked after".
☐ "Sad, scared and vulnerable nobody there for me".
☐ "Sad, scared and alone nobody there for me".
☐ "Sad nobody there to help me".
☐ "Sad, lonely and isolated Mum and Dad not there for me".

9.   Real-life Root-Cause Reasons justifying the belief
     I'm alone, lonely and/or isolated include:

☐ "Sad I'm so isolated".
☐ "Sad nobody to play with".
☐ "Lonely and isolated with no support".
☐ "Sad that I'm alone in the universe".
☐ "Sad and lonely my sister didn't want to be seen with me".
☐ "Sick, scared and vulnerable when left out and not liked".
☐ "Sad and lonely not seen or understood".
☐ "Sad and isolated when unfairly ganged up on".
☐ "Sad and helpless when people turn and walk away".

- [ ] "Left out and alone nobody to turn to".
- [ ] "Sad, lost and lonely nobody there for me".
- [ ] "Sad I had nobody".
- [ ] "Sad and lonely because I'm alone and not liked".
- [ ] "Lonely and isolated coz Mum & Dad split up"..
- [ ] "Sad, lost and alone Dad's gone".
- [ ] "Sad and vulnerable Dad's gone".
- [ ] "Lonely and isolated because I should be something else".
- [ ] "Sad Dad not there to comfort me".
- [ ] "Sad and scared people think I'm disgusting and exclude me".
- [ ] "Sad and angry when separated from Mum".
- [ ] "Scared of being alone and lonely".
- [ ] "Sad, scared and isolated because I'm fat".

10. Real-life Root-Cause Reasons justifying the belief
    There's something wrong with me include:

- [ ] "Guilty because I should have been a boy".
- [ ] "Hurt, sad and angry always told something wrong with me".
- [ ] "Sad, scared and guilty there's something wrong with me".
- [ ] "Sad and frustrated always something wrong with me".
- [ ] "Scared of being exposed as a fraud".
- [ ] "Sad there's something wrong with me".
- [ ] "Hurt, angry and guilty made to feel dirty".
- [ ] "Shame from being violated and dirty".
- [ ] "Sad, scared and vulnerable when I do something wrong".
- [ ] "Upset that I felt stupid".
- [ ] "Angry made to look stupid".
- [ ] "Sad, alone and not loveable because I'm different".
- [ ] "Sad and lonely I'm different".

11. Real-life Root-Cause Reasons justifying the belief
     I'm bad include:

- ☐ "Sad I'm bad".
- ☐ "Sad not normal".
- ☐ "Sad I'm ugly".
- ☐ "Sad and guilty I'm naughty".
- ☐ "Sad I don't deserve to be alive".
- ☐ "Sad and ashamed because I'm stupid".
- ☐ "Hurt, sad and guilty that I'm bad".
- ☐ "Hurt, isolated and alone there's something wrong with me".
- ☐ "I'm worthless compared to others".
- ☐ "Sad I'm a bad person".
- ☐ "Hurt, sad and worthless I'm not doing it right".

12. Real-life Root-Cause Reasons justifying the belief
     I'm not good enough include:

- ☐ "Sad never good enough for Dad".
- ☐ "Hurt about not being good enough".
- ☐ "Deflated that my best is never good enough".
- ☐ "I'm not good enough to meet my soulmate".
- ☐ "Sad not good enough for other people to want to be with me".
- ☐ "Sad never good enough for the people I love".
- ☐ "I'm shit and worthless compared to others".
- ☐ "Sad I'm always second best".
- ☐ "Sad and isolated because I'm not important".
- ☐ "Hurt always wrong and never good enough for Mum".
- ☐ "Sad and rejected because I'm not good enough".

13. Real-life Root-Cause Reasons justifying the belief
I've let others down include:

- ☐ "Sad let Dad down".
- ☐ "Sad and guilty that dad has never been proud of me".
- ☐ "Sad let my mum down".
- ☐ "Sad and& guilty I disappointed my dad".
- ☐ "Panic about letting Dad down".
- ☐ "Sad and guilty that I've failed and let my parents down".
- ☐ "Sad that I've let my parents down".
- ☐ "Feel really bad that I've hurt my mum".
- ☐ "Sad and guilty not there for my mum".
- ☐ "Sad I couldn't help Mum".
- ☐ "Sad and guilty I couldn't save my parents".
- ☐ "Sad that I've not been there for my mum".
- ☐ "Scared to let people down".

14. Real-life Root-Cause Reasons justifying the belief
I'm let down by others include:

- ☐ "Sad let down by the people I love".
- ☐ "Scared of being hurt by people close to me".
- ☐ "Lost, alone and let down by partner".
- ☐ "Hurt about being let down".
- ☐ "Sad and lonely nobody understood me".
- ☐ "Hurt Mum always put herself first".
- ☐ "Hurt, angry and disgusted at Dad".
- ☐ "Let down that Dad was so selfish".
- ☐ "Scared Dad wasn't in control".
- ☐ "Sad Dad never supported me".
- ☐ "Hurt and sad that Dad was mean to me".

- [ ] "Angry Dad bullied the confidence out of me".
- [ ] "Hate Dad dominating me".
- [ ] "Hurt let down by Dad".
- [ ] "Pissed off because I hate Dad's wife".
- [ ] "Angry I never got support".
- [ ] "Sad and scared Dad left me alone with Mum".
- [ ] "Hurt, stupid and worthless when brother put me down".
- [ ] "Sad, scared and alone when betrayed by partner".
- [ ] "Angry people do things I don't want them to do".

> REMEMBER: You are a good person. You always do your best. Your intentions are positive. And nothing can ever impact your loveability.

15. Real-life Root-Cause Reasons justifying the belief *It should not have happened that way* include:

- [ ] "Sad I didn't get to know my mum".
- [ ] "Sad I've wasted my life".
- [ ] "Sad my kids don't have grandparents".
- [ ] "Sad I got rid of my first baby".
- [ ] "Shame and guilt that I let X abuse me for so long".
- [ ] "Sad, lost and alone falling apart after abortion".
- [ ] "Sad Dad died before I got to know him".
- [ ] "Sad that I shouldn't have been born".
- [ ] "Sad I wasn't close to my parents".
- [ ] "Sad missed out on attention from my mum".
- [ ] "Sad he couldn't come to me for help"
- [ ] "Angry because I was forced to do things I didn't want to do".

☐ "Sad and guilty I was too busy and missed time with my child".

16. Real-life Root-Cause Reasons justifying the belief *I've lost someone/something I love* include:

☐ "Sad I lost my dad".
☐ "Sad and overwhelmed I've lost the people I love".
☐ "Sad, scared and alone when I lose the people I love".
☐ "Hurt, sad and scared that people I love leave me".
☐ "Sad I lost my brother".
☐ "Empty when I lose the people I love".
☐ "Sad, left out and lonely when people I love are taken away".
☐ "Sad and scared of losing people I love".
☐ "Sad to lose people I love".
☐ "Sad and scared everything was breaking down".
☐ "Sad and scared about losing Dad's love".
☐ "Hurt coz the people I love don't love me enough to stay".
☐ "Sad I lost my child and missed out on having a family"

17. Real-life Root-Cause Reasons justifying the belief *I feel bad for others* include:

☐ "Sad my dad was so weak and vulnerable'.
☐ "Sad and scared Dad was so pathetic".
☐ "Sad my dad is sad".
☐ "Sad and scared to see Dad hurt and vulnerable".
☐ "Tired of carrying my dad's heaviness".
☐ "Sad and scared to see Mum so weak".
☐ "Sad and guilty to see my mum hurting".
☐ "Sad and alone Mum gets upset and can't help me".

- ☐ "Sad and weak not able to help my mum".
- ☐ "Sad and scared to see Dad so ill and weak".
- ☐ "Scared of Mum being upset".
- ☐ "Angry Mum's parents hurt my mum".
- ☐ "Sad and helpless to see my dad suffering".
- ☐ "Sad and scared Mum so vulnerable".

18. Real-life Root-Cause Reasons justifying the belief *I'm not able to do what I want* include:

- ☐ "Stuck and helpless not free to do what I want".
- ☐ "Hate being told what do to".
- ☐ "Angry not able to do what I want".
- ☐ "Sad and stuck not free to be me".
- ☐ "Pissed off at petty rules".
- ☐ "Sad they don't care about what I want".
- ☐ "Hurt not allowed to do what I want to do".
- ☐ "Helpless I can't do anything to fix it".
- ☐ "Scared and powerless not able to stop bad things happening".
- ☐ "Sad and angry not able to complete my life purpose".
- ☐ "I'm frustrated that I'm not able to do what I want".

> REMEMBER: If you want to see something inspirational, then look in a mirror! You have already accomplished so much with your life. You are more confident than you think. You can do it!

19. Real-life Root-Cause Reasons justifying the belief
I'm unprotected, unsafe, weak or vulnerable include:

☐ "Sad and vulnerable Mum didn't protect me".
☐ "Lonely and vulnerable Dad not there".
☐ "Let down and vulnerable brother didn't protect me".
☐ "Scared, vulnerable and unprotected".
☐ "Sad I was violated".
☐ "Scared that people will see that I'm vulnerable".
☐ "Scared and helpless I couldn't stop them hurting me".
☐ "Scared of being exposed".
☐ "Scared and alone struggling for life".
☐ "Scared and vulnerable Dad's so unpredictable".
☐ "Hurt, scared and helpless couldn't tell him to stop".
☐ "Scared and vulnerable when out of control".
☐ "Scared and weak when people see I'm weak".
☐ "Scared left alone with nobody to protect me".
☐ "Hurt, unprotected and violated".
☐ "Sad and scared helpless and vulnerable".
☐ "Hurt and isolated not safe".
☐ "Sad I couldn't stop my dad from hurting me".
☐ "Scared of being weak".
☐ "Sad and alone nobody there to stick up for me".
☐ "Scared to be weak and crumble".
☐ "Scared of being hurt when exposed and open".
☐ "Vulnerable when I'm outside my home".
☐ "Scared of people seeing me".
☐ "Scared and vulnerable of Dad hurting me".
☐ "Scared my life is so vulnerable".
☐ "Tired of feeling suffocated and powerless".
☐ "Vulnerable when people invade my space".

- ☐ "Sad and frightened not protected by Dad".
- ☐ "Scared, alone and vulnerable nobody there to protect me".

20. Real-life Root-Cause Reasons justifying the belief
I can't stop bad things happening include:

- ☐ "Scared of being hurt".
- ☐ "Sad and scared of getting things wrong".
- ☐ "Scared to be homeless".
- ☐ "Scared I'm going to die".
- ☐ "Sad and scared to lose my safety net".
- ☐ "Scared of being stuck".
- ☐ "Scared something bad is going to happen".
- ☐ "Scared people I love could get hurt".
- ☐ "Sad and scared of being abused".
- ☐ "Scared of hurting my kids in the same way I was hurt".
- ☐ "Scared to get it wrong and hurt the people I love".
- ☐ "Scared of Mum and Dad splitting up".
- ☐ "Petrified of getting ill like my mother".
- ☐ "Scared of losing what I've got".
- ☐ "Scared of losing my mum and dad".
- ☐ "Scared that I will end up like Mum".
- ☐ "Scared I can't cope".
- ☐ "Scared of screwing up".
- ☐ "Sad and scared that I'm going to get into trouble".

REMEMBER: Holding grudges hurts the hands that hold them. You do not have to agree with the actions of others to heal your relationship with the past. Compassion sets you free!

MIND DETOX ACADEMY

MAKE A DIFFERENCE AND MAKE AN INCOME

People passionate about helping others from around the world have trained to become Mind Detox Method (MDM) practitioners with Sandy C. Newbigging.

Becoming an MDM practitioner is ideal for you if you are a life coach, counsellor, psychotherapist, health practitioner, teacher, therapist or healer of any kind and want to improve your effectiveness in helping others. You will also find this training highly beneficial if you have no previous training or experience. The prerequisite to learning MDM is the desire to help others be healthier and happier.

Training to become an MDM practitioner is easy and affordable. Included in your training investment is access to online training resources, the four-day Mind Detox Masterclass with a qualified trainer, and post-course certification support and qualification. Join the global team today. Academy training courses in Sandy's Mind Calm Method (MCM) are also available. Visit the website for details.

www.minddetoxacademy.com

Acknowledgements

THANKS to my family for your unending belief and encouragement. Special thanks, as always, goes to Bryce Redford, for being a light-hearted rock in my life.

The Mind Detox Method may not exist if it wasn't for nutritionist Amanda Hamilton originally inviting me to work with her on her detox retreats and giving me the opportunity to appear alongside her on the television programmes we recorded together — so thank you Amanda for the original introduction into mind-body detox.

Special thanks to the lovely Laura Jane Jones for the graphic design advice for the book cover and to Sasha Allenby for being a great friend and writing a fantastic forward. Thanks to Andrew and Esther Pepper for your encouragement and support.

Thanks to the Mind Detox practitioners around the world for your desire to make a positive difference. Finally, I am grateful to every person who has attended my talks, clinics, workshops and retreats. Without your courage to step beyond your challenges this book would not have been possible.

About the Author

SANDY C. NEWBIGGING is the creator of the Mind Detox Method, the Mind Calm Method, a meditation teacher, and author of several books including *New Beginnings*, *Life Detox*, *Life-Changing Weight Loss* and *Thunk!*. His work has been seen on television worldwide on channels including Discovery Health. He has clinics in the UK, runs residential retreats internationally, and trains Mind Detox practitioners via his academy. **He was recently commended by the Federation of Holistic Therapists as "Tutor of the Year."** For more information on talks and workshops given by Sandy C. Newbigging or to book him for a speaking event, please use the following contact details:

answers@sandynewbigging.com
www.facebook.com/minddetoxman
www.twitter.com/minddetoxman
www.sandynewbigging.com

Further Findhorn Press Titles

Chronic Pain and Debilitating Conditions Resolution
by Olivia Roberts

Retrain your subconscious to beat chronic illness and
unpleasant emotions with this easy, 3-step method.
With over 50 fascinating case histories, the reader effortlessly
acquires a great deal of knowledge on how to use this system.
With the step-by-step 'essential guides' for each exercise,
the reader can quickly begin to make dramatic changes to
the rest of their lives.

978-1-84409-570-4

FINDHORN PRESS

Life-Changing Books

For a complete catalogue,
please contact:

Findhorn Press Ltd
117-121 High Street,
Forres IV36 1AB,
Scotland, UK

t +44 (0)1309 690582
f +44 (0)131 777 2711
e info@findhornpress.com

or consult our catalogue online
(with secure order facility) on
www.findhornpress.com

For information on the Findhorn Foundation:
www.findhorn.org

AGH